The 6 Pillars of Intimacy Conflict Resolution:
The Secret to Breaking the Conflict Cycle in Your Marriage
© Copyright 2023 | Alisa DiLorenzo with Tony DiLorenzo

Request for information should be addressed to:
ONE Extraordinary Marriage, PO Box 721274, San Diego, CA 92172

Or email: info@oneextraordinarymarriage.com

979-8-9854176-8-5

DO CONFLICT BETTER SO YOU CAN FOCUS ON THE FUN AND NOURISHING PARTS OF YOUR MARRIAGE

The *Break the Conflict Cycle Workbook* will help you visualize what's actually happening to you and your spouse during the conflict cycle.

Grab Your FREE Workbook Today!

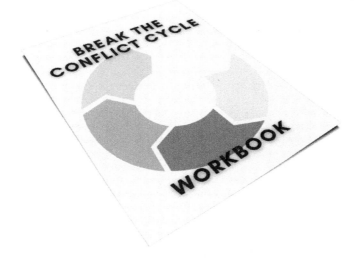

We've found readers who download the *Break the Conflict Cycle Workbook* are able to implement faster and take the next steps needed to have the extraordinary marriage they desire.

You can get your FREE workbook by visiting:
oneextraordinarymarriage.com/conflictworkbook

DEDICATION

To the couple that has thought, "There has to be a better way for us to do conflict." You are our inspiration. You are the reason for this book. Thank you for not giving up on the dream of making your marriage extraordinary.

Love you guys!

CONTENTS

A QUICK NOTE

THE VOICES IN THIS BOOK

The 6 Pillars of Intimacy Conflict Resolution was written by Alisa, so all references to I, me, my, and mine are Alisa speaking. Tony shares his insights throughout the book and we designate those with "Tony's Thoughts."

USING HUSBAND AND WIFE

Throughout this book, you will see that we use the terms "husband" and "wife," "him" and "her," and "spouses." On October 5, 1996, our wedding officiant declared us husband and wife. Spouses. This is our identity. Throughout our entire marriage, and since we began talking to couples and studying marriage in 2010, these are the words we have used.

We understand different couples use different words to identify themselves. We invite you to substitute whatever works for you, and we appreciate you allowing us to use what is meaningful to us. One of the key aspects of a successful marriage is the ability to pursue understanding, even when the two of you aren't using the same words. The same is true of us having a successful relationship with you. We might not use the same words, but the principles surrounding the 6 Pillars of Intimacy® will bear themselves out no matter what words you use.

WHY "ONE EXTRAORDINARY MARRIAGE"

The name ONE Extraordinary Marriage was the result of these two ideas:

1. Genesis 2:24: "For this reason a man shall leave his father and his mother, and be united to his wife, and they will become **one** flesh" [emphasis added] This has guided us from the beginning of our own marriage transformation. Every single day we are on a mission to help couples become one.

2. Our mission has always been to help one marriage. We figured if we could make one marriage extraordinary, it could change the world. We have been blessed to impact thousands upon thousands of marriages around the world. Each of these changed marriages leaves a lasting legacy. Yet, we know we are not done. We get up every day with the mission to impact the one marriage which needs help that day.

WHO IS THE ONE FAMILY

When we speak about the ONE Family, we are referring to the community of podcast listeners, readers, and Facebook and Instagram followers who allow us the privilege of being a part of their marriage story. We use the term family because of what it implies. Families do life together, families weather storms together, and families look for a way to make it through. Families are imperfectly perfect.

THE 6 PILLARS OF INTIMACY®

Throughout this book, I will reference the original book, *"The 6 Pillars of Intimacy: The Secret to an Extraordinary Marriage."* If you have not yet read that book, here's a quick overview of the 6 Pillars of Intimacy®, so you can understand them as they appear in this book:

- **Emotional Intimacy** is your verbal and nonverbal communication. How you talk to each other and the way you are sharing your thoughts, feelings, and desires will determine how well you can stay close and connected throughout your marriage.

- **Physical Intimacy** (different from Sexual Intimacy) is the nonsexual touch that is so powerful in maintaining your closeness and connection. Whether it's holding hands, kisses on the cheek, or a hug. This aspect of your relationship can lead to Sexual Intimacy but doesn't always have to.

- **Financial Intimacy** may sound like an oxymoron. This is the connection built from discussing every financial aspect of your marriage. It's about more than just your day-to-day finances. It includes having a plan for your accounts, insurance, retirement, and even an estate plan.

- **Spiritual Intimacy** is the way you are close and connected through your religious beliefs and observed religious practices from worshiping publicly, praying together privately, and serving together.

- **Recreational Intimacy** is part of your relationship that refers to your times of fun and leisure and how you grow your closeness and connection by spending time together and making memories. This is what the two of you do for fun.
- **Sexual Intimacy** encompasses everything about your sexual connection with your spouse. It includes romance, sexual intercourse, initiating, and foreplay.

IF YOU THINK IT'S ABUSE

It's important to note that conflict can cross the line and become abuse. This book is not intended to serve as a substitute for professional help if you are in an abusive relationship.

According to the National Domestic Abuse Hotline website, domestic violence is a pattern of behaviors used to gain or maintain power and control.[1]

Excessive conflict in a marriage can become abuse. If this is the case, please get help.

If your spouse isn't willing to get help or change and the cycles are becoming more frequent, you may be in danger. You need professional, "boots-on-the-ground" help. Not the virtual help you can get from a course or a book. This is serious and you must act to keep yourself and your children, if you have them, safe. Domestic abuse is not just punching, slapping, or kicking. Other signs of domestic abuse that show up in conflict cycles are:

- Humiliation
- Insults
- Criticism, name-calling, and shaming
- Embarrassing one's spouse in public
- Belittling a spouse's accomplishments
- Using profanity (swearing)
- Breaking things
- Preventing a spouse from leaving the room or following them around
- Not letting someone go to sleep until the argument is resolved

- Not speaking for extended periods of time
- Text fighting
- Social media posts about the spouse
- Withdrawing financial support
- Sharing unflattering or embarrassing photos or videos with others or on social media
- Being controlling, overly jealous, or possessive, monitoring the other person's behavior, reading their texts and emails, demanding all their time and attention, pressuring them to use drugs or alcohol, using social media to track their activities, trying to control who they follow on social media
- Blaming one's behavior on the spouse
- Gaslighting: creating situations where one spouse experiences confusion or questions what they have seen or heard based on the behaviors of the other spouse
- Neglect and isolation for extended periods of time
- Convincing others to turn against one's spouse
- Preventing one's spouse from seeing friends or family.

You do not have to face these things alone. Help is available 24 hours a day.

In the US: Call the National Domestic Violence Hotline at 1-800-799-7233 or visit them online at http://www.thehotline.org/ This service is available in English, Spanish, and 200+ other languages through an interpretation service.

Worldwide: Visit the International Directory of Domestic Violence Agencies for a global list of helplines and crisis centers at https://www.hotpeachpages.net/

INTRODUCTION

"Marriage is easy!"

That's what one long-married gentleman wrote on his Twitter page. His actual quote was:

"The secret to a long marriage is easy... just stay married."

How do those words strike you? Absurd? Impossible? Ridiculous? Easier said than done? Of course, anyone who has been married longer than a week knows that marriage is far from easy. It's compromise, grace, understanding, self-control, communication, and passion, and that's just the start of the list. And married people know this—it is not at all easy putting and keeping the elements in place that make a marriage work. But is it fair to only say marriage is hard? That it's constant drudgery and constant work? Or endless discussions and soul-sucking compromise? Or is marriage supposed to be a relationship where you learn how to navigate life, and where you develop skills and tools you didn't know you needed?

I would argue for the latter. What makes marriage hard might come down to a lack of skills to navigate the choppy waters of living with another human being — one who has flaws, quirks, preferences, and opinions that differ from your own. These differences give rise to conflict. And therein lies the rub. Conflict, in and of itself, is not a deal-breaker. It can actually open the door to new discoveries. But conflict poorly managed becomes a cycle of hurt, pain, fear, offense, and insecurity. Over time, most marriages struggle under the weight of repeated conflict.

I want something different for you and your marriage. In the coming pages, I invite you to look at the conflict in your marriage as a cycle, one that you can interrupt. A cycle that, once identified and understood, you can disrupt and ultimately change. If you're reading this book, there's a good chance that you know you have a cycle. But, if you're like a lot of the couples I've worked with, you don't know what to do about it. This book will change all of that.

Stop for a minute and think about those moments when you and your spouse are tip-toeing around each other, hoping not to step on one of the many landmines that explode into argument and conflict. Or, those moments that are so chilling, the two of you pull away from each other, feeling lonely and disconnected. Those times might be for an hour, a day, a week, or, sadly, forever.

Before your marriage reaches a point of no return, consider that you may lack some key tools and strategies to change direction. Many of you likely didn't learn how to handle conflict effectively while growing up, relying instead on observing those around you. By utilizing tools such as the 6 Pillars of Intimacy® framework, learning to address the tone and timing of your conversations, identifying your own conflict cycle, and breaking that cycle, you can take action to improve your marriage. Armed with these tools, you can break free from the same old arguments that never seem to get resolved and enjoy the loving connection you once cherished.

It's time for you to learn a healthy way of breaking the conflict cycle when it happens. You both deserve to have a respectful, loving marriage where each of you can hold space for different opinions, attitudes, and ways of being. And you may find that you can gain something of value when you don't agree. Learning to find the gold in disagreement without being buried by the conflict is a skill that can save many marriages from utter destruction.

OUR STORY

This cycle I am referring to is something I know from experience. Tony and I did not handle conflict well in the early years of our marriage. When we clashed, the resulting conflict was messy, uncomfortable, and unproductive.

Tony always wanted to hash things out immediately and I needed time to process or ignore the situation and hope it would go away. After several years of fights and growing disconnect, we finally had that "let's talk" conversation where we had to admit that how we were doing conflict wasn't working for us. There we were 11 years into marriage sitting in our first home, with our young children running around. We felt utterly hopeless, wondering if there was a way we could ever really be happy together. Conflict was everywhere, and we were collapsing from the pressure.

Simply put, we had three choices: 1) continue to be miserable but stay together for "the sake of the kids," 2) go our separate ways, or 3) learn how to deal with conflict better. We chose option three. But wanting to do better was not enough. How many times have you "wanted to do better" and then slipped back into your old ways? If you are like us, it's more than you can count.

We knew we needed two things to make a change: we needed to understand our cycle, and we needed clear direction on how to take action and respond differently. We also knew that we didn't know what we didn't know. So, we got busy studying our marriage, what we did, and why we did it. We looked at our friends' marriages, and eventually, we were privileged to learn from the marriages of couples in the ONE Family. We read books on conflict and analyzed what it looked like in our marriage. We tried different strategies—some that were colossal mistakes and some that were incredible successes. And, for the last 10 years, I've had a front-row seat to couples in conflict as a marriage coach.

WHY THIS BOOK NOW

In looking at these marriages, it soon became clear that couples have distinct cycles when conflict arises in their marriage. There are thoughts and behaviors each spouse engages in and they're likely to be repeated regardless of what the specific conflict is. Once a cycle is identified, then a couple can begin looking for ways to interrupt the cycle to create a different outcome. Just because the two of you have *always* handled conflict in a certain way doesn't mean that either of you can't change.

This book and the accompanying workbook are the same resources I use with coaching clients to help them understand and then interrupt their conflict cycles. Once a couple can interrupt their cycle, they can choose different actions over time to break the cycle. I wanted to make this tool available to couples even if they weren't in a coaching session. Couples can experience conflict in any of the 6 Pillars of Intimacy®, as these pillars cover everything in marriage. However, it is how they choose to communicate with one another and respond to the situation that determines if those conflicts present opportunities to grow or dangers to the health of the marriage.

Couples today are dealing with a wide range of issues. Perhaps you have concerns about how you:

- Communicate with your spouse or they with you about anything. Emotional Intimacy
- Touch (or don't touch) one another. Physical Intimacy
- Address concerns about finances (consistently in

the top 5 reasons a couple divorces).[1] Financial Intimacy

- Spend time together or if you spend time together. Recreational Intimacy
- Navigate sex. Sexual Intimacy
- Manage each other's outside interests: friends, hobbies, electronics. This could be any of the 6 Pillars of Intimacy®.

This list is not exhaustive. Rather, it's representative of some of the most common conflicts I hear in coaching sessions. You may have already thought of other issues or concerns that cause conflict in your marriage. You can add these to page 1 of your *Break the Conflict Cycle Workbook*. Grab yours for free at oneextraordinarymarriage.com/conflictworkbook.

Issues can be landmines or gold mines.

These issues can be landmines or gold mines. They can provide insight into your spouse, a different perspective, and opportunities to mature and grow. Or, they can cause your relationship to blow up. It all depends on your ability to meet conflict, face it, and steer your way through it. After all, you are different people with different backgrounds and experiences. You have a different opinion than your spouse. Whenever there is more than one person, there is an opportunity for conflict. It is inevitable. And conflict is normal. But, poorly handled, cyclical conflict without resolution can destroy a marriage.

TONY'S THOUGHTS

I was OK with conflict because it was what I had seen

growing up. Being born into a large Italian family, any time my dad and my uncles got together, there were loud voices and differences of opinion. Besides, my family had a unique dynamic—my dad and his older brother married sisters, who were twins. The twin's first cousin married another of my dad's brothers. To say our family was close is an understatement. This dynamic also meant that everyone knew everyone and how to push ALL the buttons.

Even though things got loud, very loud, and there were definitely hurt feelings from time to time, conflict growing up didn't end in divorce or anything of that nature. All of my aunts and uncles and my mom and dad were married until the day their spouse died. I didn't know any different.

Growing up, whenever my relatives would disagree, people would get over it and move on. With me and Alisa, I would get so frustrated because she would shut down or go silent and we would never come back to a conversation or resolve the issue. I had never seen anything like it. I didn't understand this dance we did or how to change it. I just knew something had to change, or we would not make it. This book is our effort to help you have the tools we didn't have, no matter what stage of marriage you find yourselves in.

It's unnecessary to debate whether marriage is hard. What is up for debate is how the two of you will handle the hard times, the times when you are in conflict. Will you choose to look at what you've always done, and what your patterns are, so you can break the cycle and do something different? If the answer is YES! then the tools and strategies you need to do it are on the following pages. But first, let's talk about your patterns, that dance the two of you do when you are in conflict.

CHAPTER 1

THE DANCE YOU DO

Husband secretly lowers the thermostat and I secretly turn it back up. We both vehemently deny touching it. Marriage is fun.

———

Stephanie Ortiz

I never thought I'd be writing a book on conflict, on the dance couples do with their conflict, or even how to break the conflict cycle. Talking about conflict isn't the "sexy side of marriage." Nobody really wants a book on conflict until things aren't going well, until the fights and the silent treatments become uncomfortable and unbearable.

When I started to see the conflict patterns in groups of coaching clients, I knew I had to write the book everyone hopes they never have to pick up. I knew that even if a couple never sought coaching; they needed a resource that could help them deal with the situations at the kitchen table, in the car, or in the bedroom. I knew I had to take what I had learned in countless coaching sessions and make it available to everyone who could get their hands on this book.

Merriam-Webster dictionary defines conflict as *struggle resulting from incompatible or opposing needs, drives, wishes, or external or internal demands.*[1] Couples experience conflict when their own ideas, habits, or opinions, are incompatible or in opposition to their spouse's. It doesn't matter if you call it arguments, disagreements, or strong and heated discussions, conflict by any name is still conflict. No matter how it plays out, the struggle, the dance couples do, keeps them out of step with each other and, more often than not, leaves them stepping on one another's toes—causing lots of pain. If the pain is too intense or too frequent, one or both of them reach a point where they want to avoid it at all costs and may choose to end the marriage.

Every couple has a dance. Maybe you're thinking of the first dance at your wedding or how you dance around your kitchen. Those are important times of connection, but the dance I'm talking about looks a little different.

It's the dance you do as you are navigating whose turn it is in the bathroom when you're running late or trying to get dinner on the table when everyone is tired and hungry. It's the way the two of you handle the chores around the house or the conversations about parenting or finances. A lot of times, the dance can feel easy, almost effortless. But, sometimes, that dance can lose its elegance and style and become a tangled clash of insults, anger, frustration, or the silent treatment. Once a cycle–your dance–has been established, it becomes a part of the way you operate. Even if it means the two of you are stepping on one another's toes and both getting hurt.

> When you have two different people, conflict is unavoidable, but how the two of you handle it doesn't have to be destructive.

If you have gotten into a dysfunctional dance in your marriage, there's a good chance you didn't notice it was happening until it was too late. By the time most couples realize what's happening, there have been years of hurt feelings and broken promises of loving, honoring, and cherishing.[2] The dance becomes a vicious cycle and it can lead to feelings of frustration, anger, or despair. In a lot of cases, couples avoid conversations to avoid conflict or even avoid their spouse because it seems easier that way. Can this ever change?

YES! You can regain your graceful dance and restore the rhythm, elegance, and style to your relationship, and it's so important that you do. Breaking the conflict cycle is, perhaps, one of the biggest keys to your longevity in marriage. Why? Research shows that the act of learning communication and conflict resolution skills has a positive impact on marital satisfaction.[3] And studies show that constructive conflict resolution is a predictor of marital satisfaction.[4] It makes sense that the more satisfied you are with your spouse, the more likely you are to stay happily married.

Most couples don't want to be married and miserable. There's a reason that "happily ever after" is associated with a wedding—it's what couples strive for. When you have two different people, conflict is unavoidable, but how the two of you handle it doesn't have to be destructive.

Divorce.com laid out the most common types of "dances" couples engage in beyond the big three - abuse, addictions, and affairs:[5]

- Clashes that result in an argument
- Lack of trust and commitment
- Issues with Sexual Intimacy
- Difficulties with communication
- Growing apart due to different values, morals, goals, and interests
- Disengagement - as in one party not helping out around the house

And in my own work as a marriage coach, these are the ones I have seen over and over again:

- Poor communication or no communication
- Disrespecting boundaries
- No sex
- Financial secrets
- Emotional infidelity
- Sexual infidelity
- Clashes over how money is earned or spent
- Not going to church together
- Issues about child-rearing/parenting
- Selfishness attitude and behaviors
- Rejection (emotionally, physically, sexually)

- Differences in values, morals, or ethics
- Different life stages
- Step-children and ex-spouse issues
- Outside influences like parents or friends
- Boredom
- Friends of the opposite sex
- Lack of goals or planning
- Time spent on social media/electronics/gaming

Any situation can be the trigger, the music that starts the dance the two of you do. It can be intentional or seemingly harmless:

Husband: *Why are you always on your phone? I can't talk to you when you're on your phone.*

Wife: *I'm just taking a few minutes for myself. What's the big deal? You get on your phone too!*

The music begins. This is the start of the fight they have had dozens of times and will continue to have if this cycle isn't broken. It is the music that sets the stage for the dance. The dance begins with a hurtful retort as they glide across the floor into position. It is followed by a rude gesture, insulting remark, or quiet disengagement that locks them in a spin that only ends when both parties are emotionally dizzy and exhausted. This couple is talking about the phone but it could just as easily be a conversation about their finances, their sex life, not getting a kiss, or even parenting.

What often fails to happen in exchanges like the one above is the couple's willingness to get in touch with what is not being said. Their focus is so intent on what they perceive their spouse is saying/doing to annoy them, they miss the subtext. Here is how that conversation might go if both parties were being honest:

Husband: *Why are you always on your phone?*

Wife: *I'm just taking a few minutes for myself. What's the big deal? Pause...*

Husband: *I was hoping we could have a few minutes to connect. Today was a crazy day and I really wanted to talk with you. I know you've probably had a full day, too.*

Wife: *(softly now) It was a busy day and I was wanting to check out and just veg for a bit. I need some time where I can do nothing and think about nothing. Give me 10 minutes and I'll come find you so we can connect before dinner.*

Imagine how differently the conversation would go if people spoke their hearts rather than spouted out from past hurts. Yet, conversations like the first scenario happen every day with couples repeating the same fights. It's like taking out the ballroom shoes, tuxedo, and gown to do the same dance again and again. It doesn't matter what the topic is, what matters is how this pattern, this cycle is repeated.

Every couple experiences conflict in some form. And conflict is not bad. As I explain in the first book in this series, *The 6 Pillars of Intimacy: The Secret to an Extraordinary Marriage,* if your spouse was just like you, one of you wouldn't be necessary.[6] The fact that you have different mindsets, energy levels, attitudes, thought patterns, opinions, etc. is not necessarily a cause for concern or the reason why you should get a divorce. It can actually be one of your greatest strengths.

Think about your favorite sports team or movie. On a sports team, you have different athletes who have different abilities ALL coming together to play as a team and to play for the win. A football team doesn't have 11 quarterbacks and no defense. A baseball team doesn't put 9 pitchers on the field without a catcher or fielders. In the same way, you can't create a movie with only actors and no writers or crew.

In each of these scenarios, it's people joining together their various skills, insights, and views to create something greater than either one could do alone. That holds true for your marriage too. You both possess different capabilities, perspectives, and opinions that can work in harmony—with a bit of practice.

There's another aspect of these examples you need to remember–many of these sports or celebrity examples have conflict, often very well publicized. It doesn't keep them from going after the goals. It's simply one more example of how all of us have to work through conflict. Just like the two of you.

Let's face it: you and your spouse are different. You have skills and perspectives that they don't and vice versa. Maybe you're a neat freak and they're a slob. Maybe you're a risk-taker and they're more cautious. These differences may have actually been the reason you fell in love and now they are the source of all your fights. Remember, at some point, those unique qualities drew you to each other. So, instead of letting your differences drive you apart, try to see them as a blessing. Embrace what each of you brings to the table and make your marriage stronger for it. Without the risk-taker, the cautious one never considers other possibilities, pushes the envelope, or presses against the boundaries. But, without the cautious one, the risk-taker runs headlong toward the cliff without checking to make sure there is a soft place to land on the other side or, at least, a parachute strapped to his or her back!

When your differences become a source of tension, conflict can arise between you and your spouse. The toll conflict takes on a marriage over time cannot be over-stated. It can lead to a lack of communication, financial secrets, less time spent together, or even a lack of Physical or Sexual Intimacy. Repeated conflict is like a cancer that destroys a marriage from the inside out.

As a marriage coach, I talk to couples daily who have been stuck in their conflict cycle for so long they are considering a drastic change—divorce. But it doesn't have to be that way. The two of you can learn to identify your dance, and your conflict cycle, and change things. But you have to know what you are dealing with, you have to identify the conflict threats to your marriage.

It's easy to wrap all of the conflicts up in one term—irreconcilable differences—and yet most irreconcilable differences are really conflicts that never got worked out, situations that were repeated over and over again until it felt like divorce was the ONLY option. It's the dance where you keep stepping on each other's toes but don't know how to change things. You can see that the two of you are hurting one another with the way things are going and yet you feel powerless to do anything different.

Being aware of the dance the two of you do is the first step to changing it. You have to know what you are doing before you can choose different actions. In working with couples since 2013, I've found one of the most powerful questions I can ask is, "What is the dance you do when there is conflict in your marriage?" In almost every single case, the couple can tell me about their dance. Likely you can too.

You know what's going to be said and how it's going to be interpreted. You know how you are going to respond and how your spouse is going to respond. You've done this dance so many times you likely don't even have to think about it anymore. How do I know? If a conflict started right now, something would happen and you would say or think, "Here we go again," or "I know what's coming next."

You can choose different actions. Your dance can be done differently. You can choose a different response… when you understand what you both learned about conflict, what your strengths are, and how the two of you process time when it comes to dealing with conflict situations. Each of these is part of the dance that's been happening up until now and they are all steps that can be changed going forward.

The truth is with skills and tools in your marriage toolbox, you can handle conflict differently and create the extraordinary marriage you desire. A marriage where your differences are no longer irreconcilable, instead they are understood and seen as strengths. Your dance can be sultry, sweet, high-stepping, or intense. With the knowledge in this book, you will find yourselves locked in each other's arms, sweeping across the floor in a beautiful dance for years to come. Yet, before you can dance gracefully you need to know where you might step on each other's toes.

Before the two of you can tackle these conflicts or others you are experiencing in your marriage, it is important to reflect on what you first learned about conflict from the people closest to you. As you'll see in the next chapter, you have to know yourself first before you can tackle the conflicts in your marriage.

GRAB YOUR
BREAK THE CONFLICT CYCLE
WORKBOOK

To get the best experience with this book, we've found readers who download the *Break the Conflict Cycle Workbook* are able to implement faster and take the next steps needed to have the extraordinary marriage they desire.

You can get your FREE workbook by visiting: oneextraordinarymarriage.com/conflictworkbook

---

If you haven't already, take a moment to download the *Break the Conflict Cycle Workbook*. This is the same workbook I use with my individual coaching clients to help them better understand *and break* their own conflict cycles.

The *Break the Conflict Cycle Workbook* will help you visualize what's actually happening to you and your spouse during the conflict cycle, and know when to stop, reflect, and redirect before a disagreement spirals out of control.

CHAPTER 2

KNOW THYSELF FIRST

Know thyself and all will be revealed.

Pamela Theresa Loertscher

L et's go back to the very beginning, a very good place to start![1]

It's easy to want to start with what your spouse is doing wrong or how they are contributing to the conflict in your marriage. Why? Well, if you're like a lot of folks, you hold your spouse to a higher standard, expecting that they should know better, or they shouldn't "think that way" or if they really knew you, the two of you wouldn't fight like this. You expect your spouse to know exactly how their words or actions are going to impact you. You say to yourself if he/she loved me they would or wouldn't do that. And then when you do something, you give yourself a pass, you lower your standards, and you justify your behavior.

This *is* normal.

And yet, it is often this very thing that causes conflict in marriage. So before you start looking at your spouse to fix everything. STOP! If you want to better understand what's happening in your marriage, you need to start with the person that stares back at you as you brush your teeth. That's the person you need to understand first. That's the person you can change. Until you get to really know him or her, the cycles will stay the same.

> No matter what you think you know about yourself, there is always more to discover.

Looking into your own behaviors through the lens of your past is a big deal. Most people don't do it because it's hard and can make you feel uncomfortable. What you discover about yourself is often insightful to the conflict cycle the two of you have. No matter what you think you know about yourself, there is always more to discover. Don't see this as drudgery. This is an amazing opportunity to take a deep dive into your life, understand who you are, and learn how to handle conflict better. The simple act of reflection can change the way you show up in your marriage. Awareness is a powerful gift to yourself and your spouse.

HOW DID THE ADULTS YOU GREW UP AROUND HANDLE CONFLICT?

(Page 2 of your workbook)

GRAB YOUR
BREAK THE CONFLICT CYCLE
WORKBOOK

To get the best experience with this book, we've found readers who download the *Break the Conflict Cycle Workbook* are able to implement faster and take the next steps needed to have the extraordinary marriage they desire.

You can get your FREE workbook by visiting:
oneextraordinarymarriage.com/conflictworkbook

Think back to your childhood and recall how the adults (parents, grandparents, or guardians) around you dealt with conflict. Try to remember a specific incident and as many details as possible. If no particular event comes to mind, reflect on how conflict was generally handled in your childhood home. Your observations about those conflicts and the emotions they stirred up within you likely reappear during conflict with your spouse.

Humans learn through observation, and what you witness can become internalized. Take the time to reflect on the conflict resolution behaviors of your parents or other significant adults in your life. What behaviors did you observe?

Some examples I've heard over the years:

- Nagging
- Yelling
- Crying
- Withdrawal
- Giving in
- Intimidation
- Manipulation
- Playing the victim
- Angry gestures
- Ignoring the other

The above list is a start. In your workbook, write down the specific behaviors you witnessed.

Now that you have thought about how people behaved around you when they were in conflict, think about how that made you feel:

- Angry at a parent(s) or the situation
- Afraid of a parent, or of you (or someone else present) being harmed
- Insecure about the relationship and the future
- Protective of a parent(s) or siblings

Looking back on your childhood experiences can shed light on your current behaviors and choices. The actions you witnessed and the emotions you felt as a child can significantly influence how you respond to conflicts in your marriage. When you recognize this connection, you empower yourself to make deliberate decisions about how to react with clarity and self-control. By acknowledging and addressing the impact of your past on your present, you can take steps toward building a healthier and more satisfying relationship.

WHAT WERE THE REGULAR THINGS THEY WOULD FIGHT OR DISAGREE ABOUT?

The topics of their fights (and yours) are very important. If money (Financial Intimacy) was an issue, there were likely fights over what you could afford or who was spending all the money. If there were disagreements over whether or not to go to church (Spiritual Intimacy), you likely heard conflict about that. If one parent wanted to spend more time with the other (Recreational Intimacy) and that wasn't happening, there's a good chance fights ensued.

It's been my experience as a marriage coach that couples tend to have conflict around some of the same things their parents did. Thinking about the nature of their fights will help you better understand the conflict in your own marriage. Often, you will see some of the same patterns showing up in your relationship.

Did you hear them fighting about:

- Money
- Work
- Lack of time spent with the family
- Housekeeping
- Extended family
- Flirting
- Affairs
- Addictions
- Personal appearance
- Disciplining and parenting styles
- Business ventures

People who grew up witnessing persistent conflict in certain aspects of their parents' relationship may unknowingly experience similar patterns in their own marriage. Although the nature of the conflict may differ, there can be subtle indications that reveal where remnants of their parents' marriage are seeping into their own. By taking a closer look and recognizing these telltale signs, you can gain insight into your own behavior and the dynamics of your marriage. With this awareness, you can take proactive steps toward breaking the cycle and fostering a healthier, more fulfilling partnership.

WHAT DID YOU LEARN ABOUT DEALING WITH CONFLICT FROM OBSERVING THEM?

As I've said throughout this chapter, the power of observation is one of the most powerful ways to learn. You create rules on how to interact with others from the lessons you observed in watching the adults around you. The human spirit is naturally wired to adapt and that adaptation comes from observation. Here are behaviors that are more commonly learned through observation:

- Ignore your emotions or choose not to express them, AKA "stuff it"
- Withdraw to get attention
- Be dramatic
- Impatience
- Raising voice
- Shutting down
- Dad has the final say
- Mom rules the house
- Don't argue in front of the kids
- Sweep things under the rug
- Pretend everything is okay until the next explosion

When you think about their fights and how they made you feel, try to remember what your inner conversation was. So many children and teenagers make promises or vows to themselves about how they will handle the same situations when they grow up. These beliefs usually start with, "When I get married, I'll never…" or "When I get married, my spouse will never…" These statements were your mental and emotional promises to yourself that made it easier for you to cope with what you saw and heard.

You might have said, "I would like to avoid doing or learn some effective new strategies around XYZ because of how they handled it." Some examples of these statements are:

- I don't ever want to be sarcastic just to make a point.
- I don't want there to be a winner and a loser when I fight.
- I'll always look for win-win solutions.
- I'll never yell in front of my kids.
- I'll never threaten my spouse or use ultimatums.
- I won't ever tolerate insults or hurtful words.
- I will never bring up the past.

You might have seen one or many of these in your family system. I would bet some of you reading this book are feeling guilty or shameful that you made those promises to yourself and broke them. If you saw one parent belittling the other, you might have promised, "I will never speak to my spouse that way." But, years later, you find yourself doing these same behaviors, maybe even saying the same words. Or, you promised yourself, after seeing your parents fight all the time, that you would "never fight in front of the kids." And yet, the two of you haven't figured out how to deal with conflict away from your children. Maybe you heard, "You always bring up the past!" and you resolved to deal with things in the moment until you didn't and now the two of you seem to always have fights that are a run-down of everything that's ever gone wrong in the marriage. Those inner vows and promises need to be addressed in order to break the patterns.

Working through conflict is a skill. Not one person is born with the ability to always do it well. When we were first married, we were what I would now call "conflict dysfunctional." Tony and I had no mechanism for resolving the issues that cropped up between us. I was raised in a family with a father who had a strong personality and a commanding presence. On the other hand, my mom avoided conflict at all costs. She was more likely to apologize and accept all responsibility in the face of a disagreement rather than discuss, defend, or argue her position. I would often hear Mom say, "I'm so sorry." It became her go-to response. When they got into conflict, my dad was direct, measured, and matter-of-fact. Mom? Well, she would retreat.

Watching this dynamic again and again for eighteen years taught me to respond to a man's authoritative tone by seeking an escape. Emotionally, I would check out. That made conflict in relationships and especially in marriage difficult. Any conflict resulted in an immediate shutdown. If you want to know how I processed conflict, it was like a California blackout, an immediate power outage!

As Tony shared earlier in the book, he hails from the quintessential Italian family. "Loud" was the name of the game much of the time. But, when there was conflict, the volume increased. Tony watched this with his parents, extended family, and friends. Hands waved, bodies were in motion, and they were louder than what I was used to. Both verbal and nonverbal cues taught the children watching that the loudest voice would win the argument. With Tony getting louder and wanting to resolve things right now and me shutting down because I needed time to process, we were a recipe for disaster. And a disaster it was!

After one of our disastrous conflicts, I retreated to the living room while Tony wanted to continue to talk. Tony followed me into the living room and sat next to me on the couch. However, in true avoidant fashion, I continued to ignore him even though he was sitting right next to me and looking at me.

Finally, we realized our approach was not working. After 11 long years, we needed to find a way to get through conflicts without getting locked in the same useless cycle. There had to be a way to interrupt the pattern and come to a different conclusion. And there was! This book and its strategies will equip you to interrupt your conflict cycle and create a different response.

Please note, this introspection and examination of the past does not have to center only on the negative. You might have seen positive attributes in your parents. There's a chance you realized there were behaviors you'd like to have in your own marriage. If you did, you might have made some promises around those functional or loving behaviors you witnessed. These might have prompted you to say to yourself, "When I get married, I will do XYZ the way they did because it was so effective." Perhaps you saw one of the following:

- One or both parents stepping away to regain control of their emotions
- One or both parents attempting to show the kids how to get to a place of conflict resolution through teamwork
- Parents having respectful conversations about disagreements

- Parents asking questions rather than pointing fingers at each other
- Obvious interest in the other expressed by a sincere apology, request for explanation, or sharing their motivation
- Voices in calm tones
- Trust and freedom to discuss anything, even the difficult topics

It's time to amplify those behaviors. What's worked for others can work for you, especially when you shift the focus from the negative to the positive approaches. By prioritizing constructive communication and conflict resolution strategies, you can foster a stronger, healthier marriage.

I NEVER SAW MY PARENTS FIGHT

You may be one of those people who never saw their parents fight at all. Perhaps they claimed they never had a fight. It is more reasonable to assume they shielded you from their conflict. This is a double-edged sword. On the one hand, not fighting in front of the kids protects them from feelings of fear and insecurity about the family structure. It can be damaging to kids when parents scream, threaten, and display high-intensity emotions toward each other when their children are in earshot.

On the other hand, it is important to learn by example the right way to enter and exit a conflict. Parents who can resolve conflict in a calm and productive manner gift their children with the tools they can use as they manage conflict both now and in the future. The challenge you are now facing in your marriage is that you have to learn how to deal with conflict well since you had no positive example to model.

This also holds true for individuals who were raised by a single parent, whether it was their mother or father. Without both parents in the home, you may not have witnessed healthy conflict resolution practices firsthand. You may have overheard one-sided phone conversations where you could only imagine the words and tone of the absent parent. If you grew up in this type of environment, you can still develop skills to resolve conflict well.

HOW DO YOU ENGAGE? FIGHT, FLIGHT, FREEZE, OR FAWN

Let's address one more aspect of conflict: your physiological response to a perceived conflict threat. When conflict is escalating, people's behavior tends to fall into one of four categories. Understanding these four can help you identify how you and your spouse are responding and can potentially change the outcome of the conflict. Let me be clear, these are behavioral responses, not an identity. It is much easier to change your behavior than it is to change who you think you are.

Fight is the reaction where people get loud, confrontational, and aggressive. Flight is when the reaction is to leave the situation as fast as possible. Freeze occurs when there's no action taken, and the spouse stops talking or even engaging with the other spouse.[2] Fawn is the reaction when you are actively seeking to appease the other person in trying to reduce conflict. You might think of this as "people pleasing."[3] In our marriage, I used to be much more of a "freeze" person, and Tony was definitely "fight." What about you? Which one did you witness, and which one looks like you today?

If **fight** is your first reaction, you can choose to take a step away and engage in breathing exercises or calming thoughts before reacting. You can even announce that you are going to walk away for a few minutes to clear your head.

For those who are more likely to turn to **flight**, you can identify what will help you stay in proximity to your spouse. It might be changing your location or focusing on an object or thoughts that help you stay engaged.

Those who have a tendency to **freeze** need an opportunity to reconnect themselves to the present situation. This can happen through breathing exercises, encouraging your spouse to ask you simple "yes" or "no" responses to re-engage you, or making simple movements to get your body out of the frozen state.[4]

Finally, if your tendency is to **fawn** over the other person in conflict, stop and become aware of what you're experiencing. How are you trying to make the situation better? What are you doing to appease your spouse without regard for yourself?

Regardless of your response type, becoming aware of it and taking action to overcome it is possible, and it will change how the two of you resolve conflict in your marriage.

In learning about these different types of responses, you become empowered to choose a different response. When you know what you do and how you respond, you can take different actions instead of just reacting or saying, "That's just the way I am." As I often tell my coaching clients, "You are not dead. You can choose different actions and different responses." True for them and true for you.

What you saw and the vows you made to yourself impact you and how you show up in conflict. Knowing what these are, "knowing thyself," is the first step to creating change. So many of the couples I've had the privilege to coach never realized they had these ingrained behaviors or scripts lurking in the shadows. They just thought the marriage was broken.

TONY'S THOUGHTS

Growing up, my father was a general contractor and often had to work long hours or even be away for weeks at a time. Although I knew there were stressors surrounding his work and our extended family, my parents shielded my younger brother and me from any conflicts they may have faced. In fact, I can't recall ever seeing my parents argue or fight in front of us. However, this led to a dynamic where my dad would avoid conflict and simply appease my mom, even if it meant giving up his own desires or plans.

One vivid memory of this had to do with building a house in another town from the one where we lived. My mom never wanted to leave the town I grew up in, even when my dad offered to build a house somewhere else. My dad didn't want the conflict, so he didn't push it and ultimately sold the property without ever building the house. That was their dynamic. As a child, my perception was that my dad would just appease my mom and avoid the conflict.

As I got older and entered my own marriage with Alisa, I realized I wanted more than just to avoid conflict. I wanted to address our issues and work toward a more fulfilling life together. At first, I struggled with how to handle conflicts in our relationship, feeling inadequate and unsure of what to do. When Alisa expressed disagreement or pushed back on something, I would challenge her instead of just appeasing her, as my father had done. While this approach wasn't always easy, it ultimately led to some of the most incredible experiences and growth in our marriage.

Reflecting on what you witnessed growing up and understanding how it has shaped your own responses to conflict can be a powerful tool in improving your marriage. By recognizing the impact of your upbringing on your communication style, conflict resolution skills, and emotional responses, you can begin to develop a deeper understanding of yourself and your spouse. By amplifying positive behaviors and transferring helpful or valuable skills from one area of your life to another, you can strengthen your foundation for a fulfilling marriage. Ultimately, by acknowledging and addressing the impact of your past experiences, you can work toward building a brighter and happier future with your spouse.

When you know yourself better, you can take steps to heal past hurts and respond differently to conflict in your own marriage. Your marriage doesn't have to be a repeat of what you saw growing up. You can do conflict differently, especially once you also understand how the two of you do conflict, as we will discuss in the next chapter.

CHAPTER 3

HOW WE SHOW UP IN CONFLICT

What comes easy won't last long, and what lasts long won't come easy.

Francis Kong

How the two of you handle conflict in any area of your marriage isn't just about what you saw growing up. While that is one critical facet, you are now adults. And whether you admit it or not, you have made many decisions about how the two of you will handle the conflict in your marriage. How well you will do as a husband or wife relies heavily on the strengths you each possess, your awareness of the areas that you want to improve, and your willingness to adopt the skills that will help you move from dysfunctional to functional.

Handling conflict is a skill. None of us is born with the wit of Winston Churchill, the charm of Nelson Mandela, and the acumen of Warren Buffett. While these folks were or are some of the greatest negotiators in history, each of them had to learn the skills that allowed them to excel in some of the worst conflicts in politics or business. So, get rid of the idea that conflict resolution skills are either something you have or you don't. Commitment to marriage and breaking the cycle of conflict is a commitment to growing in the areas that need to be developed.

It would be great if, in the dating phase, you had conversations and brainstormed exactly how the two of you would handle conflict in your marriage. Let's be honest; even if you did discuss it through your premarital counseling or conversations with others, the truth of the matter is this: everything changes after the "I do." It's easy to be so infatuated with the other person that the little conflicts of your dating days can be written off as "not that big of a deal." But time has a funny way of changing how you see those little things. What you thought wouldn't bother you does. What you

> Imagine conflict more like mining than fighting.

thought you could handle over time, you feel like you just can't anymore.

Regardless of whether you did or didn't discuss conflict, if you are reading this book, you're curious about how to change the cycle of conflict in your marriage. You want to be able to handle conflict in any one of your 6 Pillars of Intimacy® because you want an extraordinary marriage.

> If you can minimize your weakness in conflict, you can maximize your strengths and forge a stronger bond between you.

Remember, not all conflict is negative. Conflict is inherent in doing life with another person and the most tangible example of doing life with someone else is marriage. Conflict becomes dysfunctional when it is handled contentiously. But when it is handled well, it brings new ideas and better understanding.

Imagine conflict more like mining than fighting. When you mine, you have to disturb the soil, dig deeply, and move things that have been firmly in place. The goal of fighting is to have a winner and a loser. The goal of mining is to discover treasure. Conflict can help you get to the valuable core of yourself and your spouse so the union grows stronger. If you can minimize your weakness in conflict, you can maximize your strengths and forge a stronger bond between you.

STRENGTHS IN PROCESSING CONFLICT
(Page 3 of the workbook)

Strengths and conflict may seem like an oxymoron, two words that definitely don't belong in the same sentence. For so many people, conflict in a relationship seems like a sign of weakness, an indicator that something is wrong with them or with the relationship. If you and I were sitting in a coaching session right now, I would pause and ask you about your strengths when it comes to how you handle conflict.

You may not recognize them right now, but you will as you continue. How do I know? I've worked with hundreds of couples over the years and have yet to meet a person who doesn't have at least one strength when it comes to how they handle conflict.

Maybe, like some of my clients, when it comes to the conflict in your marriage you can't think of any strengths, and yet if I asked you, "What is another area of your life where you *do* handle conflict well?" You might tell me that you handle conflict well in your job, with your friends, with your kids, or even with strangers. At this point, I would ask you, "What do you do well in those situations?" And you might say, "I'm able to keep my cool," or "I don't storm out. I choose to listen even if I don't agree," or "I don't raise my voice."

Skill in one area of your life can be transferred to other areas in your marriage. Transferring skills is a powerful tool for improving your marriage. Just as skills learned in one aspect of life can be applied to other areas, skills developed in one area of your marriage can be used to improve other areas as well. For example, effective communication skills used in handling conflicts can be utilized in other aspects of your relationship, such as discussing goals or expressing appreciation for one another. By recognizing and transferring useful skills, you

> Skills in one area of your life can be transferred to other areas in your marriage.

can build a stronger foundation for your marriage and improve your marital satisfaction.

Over the last decade of coaching, I've found most people have learned to manage conflict quite effectively in public. It's a bit different though when you walk into your kitchen and have to deal with your spouse. Arguably, having a loving, functional, and respectful relationship with the person you sleep beside every night is more important than any other interaction in your world. But it's way too easy to rely on the strength of their love and commitment, and maybe take that for granted, when it comes to conflict in your marriage. You let your strengths, those excellent conflict resolution skills you use in other areas of your life, slip.

If you struggle to identify what your conflict resolution skills are, it's ok to ask your spouse or a friend. Sometimes it's hard to identify your own strengths but others see them more clearly. I've found that even in the most contentious marriages, the ones on the brink of divorce, there's still likely one quality your spouse can identify–even if it's about how you do conflict with people outside of the marriage.

You might hear things like, you are able to step away from the heat and take a minute to cool down. Or it might be that you never raise your voice when you are out in public. Some of you might hear that you are able to see things in a logical way or that you are sensitive to what others are feeling even when you are emotionally charged.

In the same way that you have strengths you can utilize when conflict occurs, so does your spouse. Now, I know that you might not always think so, but pause and think of when your spouse has done conflict well, even if that's not been directed to you. Perhaps you have seen the way your spouse negotiates a fight between two employees. Or you have seen them deconstruct an argument with the kids.

These are the same skills that can be used to soften your conflicts with each other and get to a positive resolution faster.

Own your strengths! Don't downplay them; celebrate them. When you recognize and acknowledge your strengths, you become empowered. You learn to trust your words, thoughts, reactions, and interactions with your spouse. You feel a sense of pride when you are able to see a cycle broken as you and your spouse hit those patches that once were triggers for an argument but are now managed calmly and productively.

Remember that these skills can occasionally lead to disagreements. Don't let this make you forget the fact that they are strengths. For instance, I am very detail-oriented. When Tony proposes an idea, I start breaking it down into its various components and inquire as to how it will be carried out, what needs to get done, etc. As a coach, this is incredibly useful to my clients in helping to reduce any conflicts in their marriages. It's useful when Tony and I work things out together too. However, there have been moments in our marriage where those same details have caused problems—BIG TIME. At times my "need-to-know-all-the-details" personality can be super frustrating to my "visionary-the-details-will-work-themselves-out" husband. It's still a strength. It just needs to be managed like a tool rather than as a weapon or selfish indulgence.

Husbands and wives can have different strengths when it comes to handling conflict. This is normal. In coaching couples, I've found that when a couple focuses on their strengths, it becomes easier to make changes. It's not about always being in a place of "improvement" or having to "be better." Rather, it's looking at what each of you does well, doing more of that, and then developing the other tools your marriage needs to be extraordinary.

Understanding the strengths in one another means

that you can activate those strengths when situations go sideways. What are some of the strengths you see in yourself or your spouse? Here are a few to get you started:

- Patient
- Calm
- Direct
- Solution-oriented
- Self-aware
- Analytical
- Diplomatic
- Caring

In your workbook, jot down the strengths you and your spouse have and think through how they are used, highlighting ways in which each other's strengths are a benefit in times of conflict. This is a process you can, and should, go through in different seasons throughout your marriage. You are both changing and growing and strengths change as well. You will find that, as you revisit this exercise, new strengths may emerge. Bravo! Keep at it. Take the time to grow. You'll reap the benefits for years to come.

AREAS I WANT TO IMPROVE

In any conversation about strengths, it's almost inevitable that a person also thinks about the areas they want to improve. Just in case you missed it, the heading on this area is focused on *your* personal growth, not the growth of your spouse. You can't change your spouse. They must feel motivated to do the work themselves. As you work on yourself, you create a different environment in your marriage. As you become more aware of what the conflict cycles are and how you show up, you change your reactions. And as you do, your spouse will change as they react to you.

Note: If your spouse is not reading this book with you, do not feel discouraged. Sometimes the wounds are so deep, people are afraid to touch those sensitive and tender spots again. They protect their vulnerabilities out of fear. I want to encourage those completing this process alone: do it anyway. The changes in your perspective, conflict management skills, and general sense of contentment in your marriage will be noticeable to your spouse. He or she will not be able to miss them.

You may find that your spouse asks what is going on and why you are behaving so differently. At that point, start the conversation with them about this book or about how you are approaching your conflict cycle differently. Until that time, remain diligent in the work you are doing on yourself. Stay committed and engaged in those parts of your marriage you can control. Give your spouse the opportunity to engage with you differently.

Every person is a work in progress. Each of you has something you can do better or areas that need repair. This is why understanding the 6 Pillars of Intimacy® is so important. Rather than making blanket statements like:

- My marriage is in trouble;
- I don't know what I'm doing wrong; or
- I can't read my spouse's mind to know what he/she wants;

you can examine your relationship from its most foundational aspects. As an individual and as a couple, you can look at each pillar and decide if it is still supporting the marriage well or if it has cracks and needs an overhaul.

It's normal to want an extraordinary marriage. Very few people get married thinking it won't last. Why would you do that? Why would you spend the money, time, effort, emotional connection, and a myriad of other things that go into creating a marriage in the first place if you thought it would end in divorce? Divorce is messy, expensive, and painful. People enter a marriage hoping they will be able to beat the odds and go the distance. Repeated conflicts have a way of shaking your confidence in your spouse and in yourself. You feel less secure in your marriage and worry whether the next blowup will be the end.

The assessment of yourself you have done may have prompted an aha moment where you realized that you fight about money because it was the primary source of conflict in your childhood home. Or perhaps you feel insecure because one parent or the other was always leaving after an argument for days on end and you find yourself doing the same thing. Or, sadly, you might be one of the ones who had to suffer the loss of a parent who abandoned the family after conflict broke down the union. Any of these can leave you feeling ill-equipped to operate in a healthy way when disagreements arise in your marriage.

If you're still together, it's possible to repair the broken places and move ahead. Don't worry too much about which skills you lack. Let's face it, if you were a master of these skills, you wouldn't be reading this book right now. When conflict arises and we don't know how to handle it, things can get messy. It's like the time in college when I tried to cook dinner for my roommates - nothing turned out quite right, there was food everywhere, and I dreaded cleaning it up! Conflict is just like that kitchen mess - when you don't know how to do it well, it blows up everywhere. But over time, we learn how to clean as we go and eventually learn how to minimize the messes in the first place.

So, what areas do you want to improve? Be specific. Think about the statements you've made to yourself or to friends about how you want to behave. Think about the statements your spouse has made to you about your reactions. The more specific you are, the easier it is to recognize what's not working and where you need a plan. Write those statements down.

- I need to stop using profanity when talking to my spouse.
- I need to remain engaged or ask for short breaks if I need a moment of composure.
- I need to listen and refrain from interrupting.
- I need to keep a check on my tone and volume.
- I need to remain seated and not jump up or pace around.
- I need to refrain from predicting that this discussion will go badly and trust that we will work through the issue.
- I need to process my emotions and use both my heart and head in my interaction with my spouse.
- I need to figure out what I'm feeling so I can accurately communicate my feelings and not simply rely on being angry or sad.

These are the kinds of "things to do" you can write down and focus on — one at a time. Practicing keeping your voice down, for one, is a full-time job for people who are highly expressive. But that animated style of communicating is cracking your Emotional Intimacy Pillar and possibly another pillar specific to the topic you are fighting about. So, pausing for a moment before speaking to set your tone and volume will speak volumes (pun intended) to your spouse that you are working hard to break old cycles.

This is more powerful than you can imagine. Looking at your marriage this way shifts you from battling each other and moves you into the space where you are confronting old habits, mindsets, reaction styles, etc. The fight is not with your spouse. The real battle is tearing down old paradigms and erecting new ones based on creating an extraordinary marriage using the 6 Pillars of Intimacy®.

I can and will teach you the skills. What I cannot teach you is your reason to want to try again. And it is that reason which will sustain you through the work needed to move into a new and healthier place. You can grow individually and together as you focus on those critical areas. That is how you strengthen a marriage!

WHY I FEEL FOCUSING ON THESE AREAS IS SO IMPORTANT TO OUR MARRIAGE

As you go through this process of deciding what matters to work on, remember to ask yourself why. It is your WHY that gives you the motivation to do difficult things. Why is it so important for you to break out of negative patterns in your marriage? What's making you focus on it NOW? Your reason will be what keeps you going when it's tough and exhausting. Without a solid WHY for changing this area of your relationship, you'll end up spinning in the same conflict cycles instead of pushing forward. You won't be able to sustain much inner strength and it will be easy for you to give up.

It's not enough to know what the problems are. You must also get to the why. Try this mind-blowing exercise: ask yourself why breaking old conflict cycles are important. Once you answer, ask the same question again about your previous answer. Keep going until you are at the root and cannot go any further. Here's an example:

Question: *Why is it so important to break old conflict cycles in my marriage?*

Answer: *So, we don't fight so much.*

Question: *Why is it so important that we don't fight so much?*

Answer: *Because fighting makes me feel insecure.*

Question: *Why does fighting make me feel insecure?*

Answer: *Because my parents fought so much, they eventually couldn't stand to be with each other and their marriage ended. I had to watch as my dad packed his boxes and moved. Then I rarely saw him, and it broke my heart. We were so close. I'm scared that if we stay on the path we are on that we will end up divorced and I don't want that for our marriage.*

This is a HUGE Why!

By going down, layer after layer after layer, you discover that you connect fighting to abandonment. Now you can let go of your combative mindset toward your spouse and tackle the real issue that lies at the heart of your conflict. That is how you interrupt conflict cycles!!!

It doesn't matter if you have been married for 30 days or 30 years. You need motivation to take action. Your *why* is that motivation. It's the reason you will choose to do hard things. It's the reason you will choose different actions and reactions. It's the reason you will try one more even when you're tired. If you can find the why, the how reveals itself:

- How to change my responses
- How to control my behavior
- How to express myself more fully

- How to feel comfortable asking for what I want
- How to listen actively and intently to my spouse
- How to navigate conflict to a solution rather than yet another stalemate

TONY'S THOUGHTS

Like so many couples, the first few months of Covid lockdowns were hard for us. In December 2019, I sold my paintless dent repair business. This had been my identity for 22 years. When I had that business, I would leave the house every day and be away from Alisa and the kids. If we'd had a fight or were dealing with things, I could get out and deal with it, process it on my own. Come March 2020, everyone is home. Alisa and I are navigating ONE Extraordinary Marriage in unprecedented times and I'm scared. Scared that we are going to repeat losing everything as we did in the Great Recession.

In the midst of this, Alisa and I were having a conversation about what to do next. Alisa's strength is the details and mine is the vision, the big picture. I have a tendency to throw things out there not knowing if it's going to work or not. Because we are partners in life and business, it's important for Alisa to also be on board, so it's not just me making unilateral decisions. We were in my office and I'm offering suggestions to Alisa and she started asking questions. SO. MANY. QUESTIONS… about all the little details.

I felt stuck, trapped even. And she wanted to dig into the smallest details of every single thing I was suggesting. I didn't care that details were her strength. At that time, it felt like the biggest pain in my butt. I felt attacked. I didn't feel supported. I needed my business partner. I needed my wife to encourage me and Alisa wasn't offering any of that.

I walked out of the room and, for the first time ever, and since, I gave Alisa the silent treatment. It took us almost 24 hours to actually be able to circle back around and both be in a place where we could have a conversation about the emotions behind what had happened. I knew we had to resolve this because one of my big reasons for learning to do conflict well is that divorce is not an option for us. We have to work things out.

We've talked about your dance, understanding yourself, and evaluating how the two of you show up in conflict. There's one more key area we need to talk about before we can talk about breaking the conflict cycle and that is how the two of you process time when you are in conflict. You've likely already figured out that what you need in terms of time is different when you aren't getting along. This is why we need to talk about that before we talk about breaking the conflict cycle.

CHAPTER 4

THE CLOCK IS TICKING

Remember that creating a successful marriage is like farming: you have to start over again every morning.

———

H. Jackson Brown, Jr.

Pause for a moment and listen. Do you hear it? It's the tick–tick–tick of a timer that is about to release the deafening sound of a ringing alarm. Or maybe you can imagine the theme music from "Final Jeopardy" playing to remind you that you only have a few seconds left. I bet you can hear it now. And, if you can hear it, you likely also feel the pressure building. As it continues, you probably have one of two wishes: Ding the bell right now or have the timer extended.

Time is the great equalizer among us. It is something that places us all on even footing. Everyone gets 24 hours a day whether you are rich or poor, old or young, no matter where you live. The rich cannot buy more hours and the poor cannot sell theirs. Time is the same for us all unless a husband and wife are in conflict and then time seems like a tug-of-war. One person wants to solve or fix things NOW and the other needs time to process what's going on.

Time in conflict refers to two things: the time needed by each spouse to process the situation and their emotions AND the timing of the conversations the two of you have. If you can crack the time code in your marriage, you can change so much about how the two of you handle conflict. By understanding how both of you view time in conflict, you can manage expectations and create solutions.

As a marriage coach, it's probably no surprise to you that a LOT of my coaching sessions deal with conflict situations. Over time, one of the patterns I started to see was there was often one spouse who wanted to process everything "right now!" Let's do this quickly and get it over with—the "fast processor." And the other spouse who wanted time to process their emotions, think about the situation, and calm down—the "slow processor." The terms "fast" and "slow" simply refer to the speed at which you process the situation and your emotions. There is no right or wrong way to process emotions, rather, the understanding of how you each are wired allows for growth in how you do conflict. When you understand this dynamic in your marriage, you can move toward understanding more smoothly.

What does it look like for each of you to develop an understanding of how your spouse is wired *and* give your spouse what they need to come to a resolution? I'm glad you asked. Learning how your spouse is wired and what they need is a way of showing them love and respect. Yes, there are issues that require a decision right now. In the same way, there are other times when there is enough of a window that you can take time to process. The challenge is knowing who your spouse is and what they need in order to be able to get to a place of calm and resolution.

If you are a "fast" processor married to a "slow" processor, your gift is *the gift of time.* When you allow your spouse time to get their thoughts in order, time for their emotions to settle, and time for them to understand the situation, you are demonstrating your understanding of who they are. If you are a "slow" processor married to a "fast" processor, your gift is *the gift of re-engagement.* When you come back to the conversation after you've had time to process and don't avoid talking about the topic, you express your love to your spouse in closing the circle.

When this doesn't work, you have the "fast" processor wanting to resolve everything right now. They don't want to give their spouse time to process. They don't want to wait for emotions to settle because they are afraid if they allow the conversation to stop, and their spouse to step away, they'll never come back to it. They are afraid there will never be a resolution. The "fast" processor may develop the habit of forcing the conversation. The spouse who needs time may get into a place where they say anything to simply end the conversation, even though things aren't resolved. On the other hand, the "slow" processor may be the type of person who asks for time and then doesn't come back to the conversation. There's no resolution; the conflict simply gets swept under the rug, avoided, or ignored.

Now, you can have two "fast" processors or two "slow" processors married to one another. It does happen. When two "fast" processors are married to one another, everything gets dealt with "in the moment;" however, words can come flying fast and furious so it's important to be mindful of your words and emotions. In some instances, the "fast" processors may not even be aware of what they are truly feeling until after some time has passed, or things have settled down. If this is the case, then it's important to circle back to your spouse and share what you've learned about yourself. If two "slow" processors are married to one another, conflict can linger without any resolution because there is no plan to re-engage. Both of you go to your quiet place and think things through. It is important in this scenario to have a plan for re-engagement.

In each of these scenarios, at least one spouse can find themselves frustrated, walking on eggshells, angry, etc. What the two of you need in terms of time, is one of the keys to breaking the conflict cycle in your marriage. When you give time or re-engage, you build trust in one another and in the relationship.

Now, if there are situations when your processing time changes, this is important to discuss with your spouse. If finances are a hot topic and you always want to discuss it "right now," but parenting topics need a bit more advance notice, this is important to share with your spouse.

Time is also about the timing of your conversations. Timing asks if the conditions are optimal to discuss a topic. You know that moment… a conversation starts and all you can think about is why this is a bad time. Perhaps a crowded restaurant on a Friday night over dinner is not the right time to ask a loaded question about family. Similarly, lying on the beach in Cancun may not be the right time to talk about being over the limit on a credit card. Often, couples will address issues when they come home at the end of the day, tired, frustrated, and hungry. Or they will try and have the conversations at the end of the night when everything else is done and you both want to just fall asleep. I have shared with so many couples over the years that it's hard to have a productive conversation that doesn't lead to conflict after 9 o'clock.

It's OK to say, "This can't be done now. I want to give you my full attention." Or, "I don't have the capacity to talk about this right now. Let's figure out a better time to talk about it." This type of statement acknowledges that what your spouse brought to you is important and that you want to be able to give it your full attention. You might wonder then what is the right time? To be clear, I'm not talking about urgent matters that require an immediate text or phone call. Things like, "Honey, I have a flat tire. Can you pick up the kids from school?" Or, "The water heater just stopped working, can you call me?" When I talk about scheduling time to talk, it's about those topics that need your full attention and need time, topics like finances, parenting, family, emotional concerns, etc. With these types of topics, it's important to have a set time every day or every week to discuss what's going on with both of you.

When you know that time is on the calendar, you don't have that same sense of needing to address it "right now" or as soon as someone walks in the door. This scheduled time allows you to write down (or make a note in your phone) the topics you want to discuss and your thoughts about them. This keeps you from feeling that overwhelming sense of "I don't know when we are going to talk about these things." Some couples do this as part of their walk and talks, their drive and dives, or their weekly marriage meeting. When you know there is a time to discuss the things that are important to you, you can reduce the conflict and anxiety of not knowing when you will be able to talk about these topics.

Setting or environment is a big part of timing. Many couples find themselves in conflict because they always talk about the same topics in the same place. Think about it. Do you talk about sexual issues in your bed right before sex? Do you discuss finances at the dining table right after dinner? Are the parenting conversations taking place in the kitchen when you are trying to get food on the table or when the kids are around? Just because you've always had those conversations at those times and in those places doesn't mean you can't change it up.

Choosing to change the setting will change the timing of when you deal with the challenges in your marriage. Go on a long drive through the countryside to talk or take a walk in a park or the botanical gardens to discuss something sensitive. If you are blessed to live near water, there are few things more calming than walking by a river or along the beach.

HOW WILL WE KNOW WHEN IT'S TIME TO RE-ENGAGE

If you table a topic with the intent of talking about it at a better time or in a better environment, be sure to discuss **how** the two of you will re-engage. This is key for the "slow" processor to share with the "fast" processor. Some people can use the gift of time as an excuse not to engage in the hope the topic will be forgotten or that it will be replaced by more pressing concerns. This is not fair to you, your spouse, or your marriage.

Remember, if you are the person who needs time to process, your spouse is waiting for you to come back for discussion. They have gifted you time to process. Gift them your willingness to return to the conversation. This is an opportunity to build trust and change the way the two of you do conflict. Your spouse is trusting that you are not going to bury this and will re-engage later. As you continue to come back to these conversations, your spouse will be more willing to accept that space is needed. You trust them to let you disconnect from the conflict for a moment, and they trust you to come back at the predetermined time.

Here is how Tony and I ensured we would reconnect to discuss an area of conflict. For us, "walk and talks" have been a great time to reengage. This understanding happened totally by accident. But, looking back, it was a great breakthrough in our marriage. The walk got us out of the house, which we want to be a place of peace and calm. Walking provided us with a change of scenery. We could go anywhere we wanted to go in order to talk. And walking ensured we had privacy to work things out. Now, sometimes we still deal with conflict in our home because we want our children to see and hear a healthy model of handling marital conflict. But, when a discussion is especially tense or difficult, walks have been a haven for us. And they provide the perfect framework for our re-engagement sequence. If a conflict needs space and time, we simply make plans to get out and go for a walk. That could be later in the day or the following day. Over time, we've built trust in one another so that we can both allow the conflict to rest until we are ready to go for a walk.

TONY'S THOUGHTS

One of the key things I have learned over the years is that it's important to my marriage that I love Alisa enough to understand she isn't going to always get to a resolution at the same pace I do. Sometimes she's quick and decisive, yet in other situations, especially when it comes to situations that might have bigger consequences, her thought process goes in slow motion. Because of this, she needs time away to think about it, pray, feel her emotions, address her own resistance, etc. She needs space. Trying to keep her in the conflicts only hurts the situation.

Even though I may still be upset and still in the moment, learning that I can let her go and she will come back, has been a game changer for our marriage. It's still sticky, there's still tension, and yet it's knowing we have committed to being on the same team. This isn't going to end our marriage. We need time in our own space to process, calm down, get out of "flight or fight," or in her case "freeze," and de-escalate so we can come to a place of resolution we can both accept. We're not perfect. I'd say we get here 80% of the time and the other 20% we have to work through our stuff. I don't expect us to be conflict-free. If we didn't have conflict, I'd worry that we weren't connecting or sharing our true feelings.

Our understanding of time was a major breakthrough in our marriage. Once we figured out that the processing speed for each of us was different, we were able to give each other space to process in our own way and at our own speed. Now that you understand what you learned about conflict, how you show up in conflict, and what processing time looks like, it's time to jump into the circular nature of the conflict cycle.

CHAPTER 5

OUR CONFLICT CYCLE

To be fully seen by somebody, then, and be loved anyhow—this is a human offering that can border on miraculous.

▬▬▬

Elizabeth Gilbert

I f you are like many couples I have worked with, there are patterns to your conflicts. Perhaps there are certain issues you always fight about, certain actions that seem to trigger fights, or certain pillars of intimacy that are more prone to conflict than others. These conflicts often follow the same trajectory, and couples could almost write a script for them. In fact, I often ask my coaching clients to describe their conflict cycle—the dance they do when things get uncomfortable in the marriage. Every single one of them can do this.

Unpacking your conflict cycle is the first step to understanding and ultimately changing how you do conflict in your marriage. Your conflict cycle is like a story with a prologue, act one, rising action, climax, and resolution. You might tell the story a little differently each time, but it usually follows the same plot and almost always ends the same way. This chapter will provide an overview of the conflict cycle and each of its components. Knowing what you do is the first step to changing this cycle in your marriage.

The entire conflict cycle looks like this:

Every (yes, every) couple, has a conflict dance, a cycle they start when there is a difference of opinion, a mis-communication, or unmet/unvoiced expectations in any one of the 6 Pillars of Intimacy®. Being able to diagram what happens is the first step to being able to under-stand what your particular dance is AND being able to interrupt a cycle that isn't working. Begin with 'Conflict Starts' on the right-hand side and move clockwise.

What do you notice first about the conflict cycle? If you said, "It's a circle," you are correct. It is presented as a circle because this is the way conflict moves. Sometimes it can be a quick spin and then back to the status quo or a resolution. Other times, it can spin like a tornado, leaving you disoriented and unsure of how to break the cycle. At the same time the two of you are interacting with one another, there is an internal cycle that happens. The cycle happening inside you collides with the cycle happening inside your partner. The clash of those op-posing forces can create untold damage.

The clear spots between each section are the transi-tions between one phase and another. These are the op-portunities for the two of you to interrupt the cycle—opportunities to choose different actions and reactions to change the outcome.

If you've been married for any length of time, you know that failing to actually resolve conflicts, and just returning to the status quo, will result in those conflicts resurfacing again and again. Old fights from weeks, months, or even years ago can suddenly reappear and become part of the cycle of the current conflict. All the issues you have ever had conflicts about may suddenly become relevant and resurface.

As you begin to work through this cycle, choose the same situation in the center so the two of you are comparing apples to apples. A situation may simply spring to mind or you can think of one of the 6 Pillars of Intimacy® (Emotional, Physical, Financial, Spiritual, Recreational, and Sexual) and the conflicts that present themselves in any of those as your situation.

Work through this individually—this is not a group exercise—the "my reaction" refers to your own personal reaction, and the "your reaction" is there for you to share your perception of your spouse's reaction. After you have both diagrammed the conflict, you can see the patterns that emerge and better understand what is happening in your marriage. In this chapter, you'll see each phase presented in four ways: a description of the phase, an opportunity for you to reflect on your reaction and what you see in your spouse, an evaluation of your own internal cycle, and an opportunity for you to think through what you can do in this stage to interrupt the cycle.

PHASE 1: CONFLICT STARTS
(Pages 5 and 6 of your workbook)

The conflict begins with the initial moment where you realize you and your spouse aren't on the same page or the atmosphere suddenly shifts. In this situation, take note of your reaction and your spouse's reaction. For instance, if you choose a scenario like, "He forgot to tell her something important," or "She spent too much money at Target," observe how you respond and what you perceive in your spouse's reaction.

CONFLICT STARTS

my reaction

your reaction

SITUATION

WHAT IS MY REACTION? WHAT IS YOUR REACTION?

How do you recognize when you and your spouse are in conflict? What are your typical reactions, and what do you observe in your spouse? As both a wife and a coach, I've noticed certain expressions, gestures, statements, and actions often indicate the start of conflict. It could be a slightly elevated voice, an eye roll, a big sigh—what do you experience and what do you see in your spouse? Be honest with yourself and don't try to write down *how you wish you would respond or how you think you should respond.* This is all about the reality of the situation.

At the end of this exercise, you'll have an opportunity to deepen your Emotional Intimacy through discussion and truly understand how your spouse perceives conflict in your marriage. This is not the time to debate whether their assessment is true or not. Rather, it's a chance to step outside of your individual world and into the larger world of your marriage, where you can see how your actions affect your spouse. You'll gain clarity about what your spouse thinks you're thinking or how they interpret your reactions, which is incredibly useful information. Couples often repeat their conflict cycles because they haven't stopped to analyze how their behavior affects their spouse.

WHAT DO I EXPERIENCE INTERNALLY WHEN WE ARE IN CONFLICT?

Your internal conflict cycle happens at the same time the two of you are in conflict. Conflict isn't just what happens between the two of you; it's also experienced internally. In every phase, you are thinking and reacting to the dynamic happening in your environment. For many people, this is so automatic they aren't even aware of what they are thinking or doing. It's the dance that "just happens."

Most people don't spend as much time reflecting on what's happening inside of them. It's too easy to focus or fixate on what your spouse is doing. It takes courage to look inside, and when you do, the insights can be game-changers in how you handle conflict. The knowledge about how you react, what you see in your spouse, and what you are experiencing internally— allows you to step into a place of action. Let's start at the beginning.

MY INTERNAL CONFLICT WHEN CONFLICT STARTS

When conflict starts in your marriage, what do you think and what do you experience? This may be the first time anyone has ever asked you to really think about your response to conflict. Your thoughts are as powerful as the body you have. When you begin to analyze your responses to stress, especially the stress in conflict within the marriage, you will be able to develop an awareness that allows you to take action.

When it comes to the thoughts you have when conflict starts here are some I hear in coaching sessions:

- Oh no, what did I do wrong?
- Here we go again.
- Why can't we ever get along?
- Why is this coming up again?

These thoughts can put your body on autopilot where the physiological responses just get fired up. Some people will begin to clench their jaw or grind their teeth. Others will feel the tension creep up the back of their neck or seep into their stomach. For some, it's sweaty palms or perspiration in the armpits. Knowing what you are thinking and how your body is responding can become a way to interrupt the conflict in this first phase. Think of these internal reactions as warning lights that mean something needs attention.

WHAT CAN I DO IN THE CONFLICT STARTS PHASE?

One way to address conflict when it starts is to recognize it through your thoughts or physiological response and call it out in the relationship. This can involve asking questions like, "It feels like something is different, what just changed?" or "I recognize that I'm responding as if we are in conflict. Is this about me or is something else going on here?" By doing so, you give your spouse the gift of awareness to address things at the onset.

Understanding how the two of you respond when conflict starts is the first opportunity to break the conflict cycle. For instance, if you know your folded arms intimidate your spouse and contribute to escalating the situation, you might think twice before assuming that posture. Or, if you learn through this process your spouse always feels like they are in trouble when you bring something up, you can address that from the beginning and say, "I want to talk to you about something. I want you to know that you're not in trouble." Many coaching clients have used the knowledge from this first step to break the conflict cycle early on. However, it's important to note that conflicts may not always be resolved quickly, and sometimes require more time and effort.

PHASE 2: ESCALATION

After the initial phase of conflict, if the situation is not resolved or if you cannot reach a peaceful state, you may notice the tension starts to escalate. Some people even describe this phase as feeling like they are escalating. At this point, the situation is not yet out of control, but both parties may feel uncertain about how long they can keep things from boiling over.

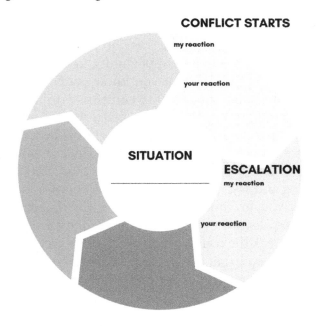

WHAT IS MY REACTION? WHAT IS YOUR REACTION?

During this escalation phase of conflict, communication tends to become more directed and hurtful. Body language can also become more aggressive or one person may start to withdraw. The focus of the conflict shifts from the original problem to personal attacks. It's important to reflect on how you and your spouse react during this phase. Do tears start to flow? Do you or your spouse use hurtful words?

Being aware of these behaviors can help you both to take a step back and de-escalate the situation before it gets out of control. It's important to consider how you can approach the situation differently, such as using "I" statements instead of blaming or attacking your spouse. Or being mindful of your tone of voice.

WHAT DO I EXPERIENCE INTERNALLY WHEN CONFLICT ESCALATES?

At this point, you likely feel your blood pressure start to rise, maybe your jaw starts to clench even tighter, or you get that uneasy feeling in the pit of your stomach. The one that says, "Oh no, this is not going to end well."

What are the scripts or statements you are making about your spouse? Things like:

- Why are you saying these things to me?
- Watch your tone. Don't speak to me that way.
- Lower your voice.
- You always/never do this.
- Why can't you just let the past be the past?

Those thoughts, because they happen so quickly, can change your attitude immediately and put you in a place where you forget this is a person that you love, a person to whom you've committed your life. It is important to remember that you are still in control of your responses.

WHAT CAN I DO IN THE ESCALATION PHASE?

When this happens, questions are better than statements. Some great questions to ask are:

- *What are we really fighting about?* Start by asking yourself this question BEFORE you ask your spouse. Often, conflicts stem from underlying issues such as financial stress, parenting disagreements, work-related tension, or situations that have not been resolved. It's important to identify the root cause before discussing the problem with your partner. As the conflict escalates, it can be easy to lose sight of the real issue at hand, and instead, focus on personal attacks and blaming. By reminding yourself of the true source of the conflict, you can work toward finding a solution rather than allowing the conflict to continue to gather energy.

- *Do you have the capacity to have a conversation about this right now or do you need to take some time to process/cool down?* It's important to acknowledge that you and your spouse see things differently during a conflict and need different things in order to emotionally process it. Remember the importance of timing we discussed in Chapter 4. It's crucial to find out if your spouse is emotionally ready to work on a solution. If they're not, pushing for it can do more harm than good.

- *What do you need from me at this moment?* The two of you are on the same team. By asking your spouse what they need from you at that moment, you can work together to find a solution that benefits both of you. Teams are not successful when they tear each other down and are unable to support one another. Serving each other in moments of tension can be an incredibly effective way to break through challenges and come together as a strong and supportive team. By actively working to address each other's needs in moments of escalation, couples can shift the impact conflict has on the marriage, and even reduce the intensity of the conflict itself.

PHASE 3: THE BOILING POINT

When a conflict doesn't get interrupted in the escalation phase, it's likely to reach a tipping point where one or both partners feel like they are about to lose. The intensity of the conflict can be like an erupting volcano or a frozen iceberg, where anger, resentment, fear, or other strong emotions are either simmering below the surface or exploding outwardly. At this point, it can be difficult to find a resolution that feels fair or satisfying for both partners. It's important to recognize when a conflict is reaching this boiling point.

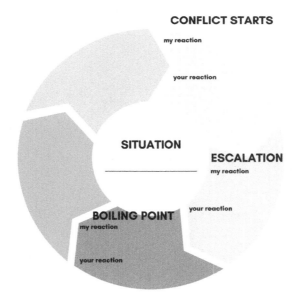

WHAT IS MY REACTION? WHAT IS YOUR REACTION?

Whether through words or actions, both parties become locked in combat at this stage. Those who explode are in full blast while those who are shut down can become completely frozen. The damage done to the marriage at this point is real, and words are often spoken that cannot be taken back. This is where insults, accusations, and threats are hurled, and where scars are left. Just like how boiling water touching the skin damages it and leaves a scar, the boiling point in a relationship damages the marriage and leaves a scar on both partners.

During the boiling point phase, some individuals resort to destructive behavior, such as hitting walls or breaking things. Others may leave the room or the house without saying where they are going, while some may resort to name-calling or swearing. The tension, anger, and frustration are heightened, and it can feel like only one person can come out on top. Extreme language often shows up in this phase:

- "I can't win with you!"
- "There is just no pleasing you!"
- "You find fault with everything!"
- "I'm so frustrated!"
- "I can't talk to you!"
- "You always…"
- "You never…"

Don't let the metaphor of the boiling point mislead you into thinking that icebergs are less harmful than boiling water. Just as boiling water can scald, so can dry ice. It can burn if touched without protection, and when the lid is lifted, steam rolls out as if it's boiling. This is the impact of the partner who completely shuts down and disengages.

Keep these images of what happens at the boiling point phase front and center. Let the picture of the scalding water or freezing iceberg stay top of mind. Awareness is critical when you are in the boiling point phase.

When you become aware of the physiological and emotional responses you are having in this phase, you can take action to answer the "What Can I Do?" question.

Please note that abusive language is never acceptable and will never be forgotten by your spouse. The same is true of physical destruction or abuse. Both verbal and physical abuse leave forever marks on the two of you. Learning to develop self-control, when you feel out of control, is a gift you give to yourself and your marriage.

WHAT DO I EXPERIENCE INTERNALLY IN THE BOILING POINT PHASE?

At the boiling point, couples can become so emotionally charged they lose much of their ability to reason and process. It's common for individuals to say things they shouldn't or describe the situation as feeling like they're "seeing red." The intensity of the situation can make it feel like they're headed over the edge quickly. This is the phase where folks ask:

- "What's wrong with us? Do we really belong together?"
- "Is it always going to be this way?"
- "Why can't we figure this out?"
- "Why do we fight every day?"

Doubts and negative thoughts start swirling in the boiling point phase. It can be a time of hopelessness, despair, hurt, and loneliness for both spouses. Many people question why they ever got married to their partner in the first place during this phase. The intensity of the conflict and the hurtful words spoken can lead to doubts about the future of the relationship, including thoughts of separation or divorce. *You aren't the first person to think this. Tony and I have had these thoughts many times over our years of marriage.* What matters is what you do when you feel this way.

Your body can feel like it's in the full "fight/flight/ freeze/fawn" mode as the stress of the situation overwhelms your body systems. This is the phase when the stress hormones adrenaline and cortisol are flooding your body and trying to protect you. You may find there are times when you can't hear your spouse, you can't think straight, or you can't seem to control your emotions. In this heightened emotional state, your body is simply trying to survive.

> You do have some control over your feelings; you just don't always exercise that control.

WHAT CAN I DO IN THE BOILING POINT PHASE?

Just as awareness is important when it comes to the impact your behavior at the boiling point has on your spouse, awareness of how to exit the boiling point phase is also crucial. You might feel like you're so angry or overwhelmed you can't calm down, but that's not entirely true. If your favorite celebrity, your best friend, or even your boss suddenly appeared in front of you, you'd likely be able to shift your mood quickly and calm yourself down. This demonstrates that you do have some control over your feelings; you just don't always exercise that control.

So, let me ask you a question. What helps you regain emotional control and the ability to have a calm conversation with another human being when you've gotten this mad?

- Do you need to exercise to release all of the energy about the situation?

- Is it important for you to be able to journal your thoughts and feelings so you can process them?
- Does changing the scenery (going for a walk or a drive) help you to regain your perspective?

To effectively manage conflict in your marriage, it's essential to know the answers to questions of what each of you needs in order to feel heard and valued. This knowledge can empower you to ask for, or offer, what is most effective when conflict arises and prevent the situation from escalating to a boiling point. When you reach the boiling point, being aware of these answers can help you choose the most effective way to communicate and handle the situation.

PHASE 4: COOL DOWN

This is the time between the boiling point and resolution, where emotions are still activated but not as heightened. It's that "in-between" time when the two of you disengage from one another. It may be that one, or both of you, retreat to your separate spaces or otherwise engage in behavior designed to lower your emotional temperature. During this stage, it's essential to give yourself and your spouse space to cool down and reflect before trying to resolve the conflict.

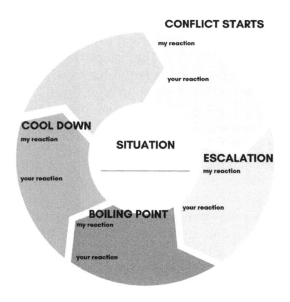

WHAT IS MY REACTION? WHAT IS YOUR REACTION?

As you work to lower your emotional temperature and figure out what just happened, you might engage in behaviors like crying, leaving the house for a change of scenery, journaling, exercising, or other blow-off-steam activities. For example, I once worked with a couple where the husband built a man cave as his place to cool down, while the wife went into "spite-cleaning mode," furiously cleaning the house to release steam. Despite the physical or emotional distance, the cool down phase is still emotionally charged, often with feelings of loneliness, anger, and defeat.

WHAT DO I EXPERIENCE INTERNALLY IN THE COOL DOWN PHASE?

During this phase, it's common to experience tears, anger, withdrawal, or even the "silent treatment." As one of my coaching clients recently shared with me, "There are times when things get so overwhelming, I just need some time to myself to calm down before I can engage in a constructive conversation. My thoughts are all over the place about myself, our marriage, and what has just happened. Taking a step back helps me sort through my actions and reactions before I can even think about approaching my spouse again."

The cool down phase is typically characterized by introspection and emotional processing. No one enters into marriage with the expectation of ongoing or repetitive conflict. Most people desire a peaceful marriage with deep Emotional Intimacy. This phase presents a valuable opportunity to evaluate what happened and identify ways to make positive changes going forward.

It's during the cool down phase that you can find yourself asking questions like:

- How did we get here?
- Why do we always seem to be fighting about these things?
- What do these fights say about our marriage?

- How do we break this cycle?
- What could I do differently?

WHAT CAN I DO IN THE COOL DOWN PHASE?

The cool down phase presents an excellent opportunity for self-reflection. It's important to remember that both spouses contribute to any fight in a relationship since you can't argue with yourself. Therefore, during this time, it is essential to look inward at your part in the conflict and examine the dynamics between you and your spouse. This introspection can help you recognize where changes need to be made to better your relationship down the line. Remember, change occurs when you each take responsibility for your actions and work together to create a better future.

- What was my role in this conflict?
- What questions could I have asked to get more clarity on the situation?
- What did I choose to ignore in regard to my spouse?
- How did I respond to my spouse's words?
- What could I have done differently in reacting to them?
- What patterns do I see in my/our behavior?

Achieving insight into your own actions is essential if you want to make constructive changes in your relationship. Taking time to look at past occurrences and acknowledging your role in any disputes can help you find solutions and to adjust your behavior accordingly. Knowing yourself better makes it possible to develop your relationship and avoid similar issues arising in the future. If you take responsibility for yourself and strive for increased self-awareness, you can create a deeper connection with your spouse.

PHASE 5: RESOLUTION OR RETURN TO STATUS QUO

At the end of the conflict cycle, there are two possible outcomes: an agreement is reached or the disagreement is pushed aside and the pre-conflict status quo is restored until another conflict arises. While not every conflict will reach a resolution, it's important to strive for a win-win outcome whenever possible. The ideal is to find a mutually beneficial solution that addresses the underlying issues and promotes greater understanding and communication. This can help to prevent future conflicts and improve the overall health of the relationship. It's important to approach conflict with a mindset of openness, curiosity, and a willingness to work toward a positive outcome for all parties involved.

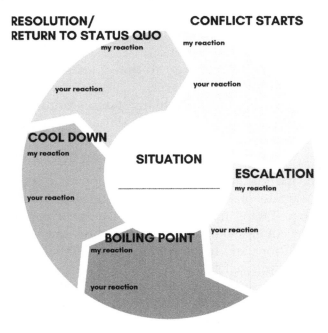

WHAT IS MY REACTION? WHAT IS YOUR REACTION?

This is a crucial moment in the relationship, where a couple can either return to the status quo or take steps to create positive change going forward. One common scenario is the decision to ignore what happened and pretend like nothing has changed. Many couples fall back into familiar patterns of behavior, avoiding the underlying issues and failing to address the root causes of the conflict. You repeat what you don't repair.

> You repeat what you don't repair.

However, when a couple is committed to finding a resolution, this phase becomes fertile ground for growth and transformation. It's a time for asking questions, initiating physical touch, and engaging in open and honest communication. This willingness to seek understanding and devise a plan for doing things differently next time can be a literal game-changer for couples.

In this phase, it's important to take responsibility for your role in the conflict and work toward a mutually beneficial solution. This may involve offering an apology, expressing your feelings, or actively listening to your partner's perspective. By working together to find a resolution, you can strengthen your relationship, deepen your Emotional Intimacy, and prevent future conflicts around the same topic from arising.

WHAT DO I EXPERIENCE INTERNALLY IN THE RESOLUTION/RETURN TO STATUS QUO PHASE?

What you experience is very dependent on the path the two of you take. If you find there's a return to the status quo, you may feel defeated, resigned, or frustrated. Questions may arise like:

- Why can't we ever seem to solve this problem?
- Is this as good as it gets?
- I wonder how long things will be good *this time*?

The questions that arise in the aftermath of a conflict can slowly erode the foundation of your marriage, causing cracks in all of the pillars of intimacy. It's crucial to consider what it would look like to move beyond simply returning to the status quo and toward true resolution. What purpose does it serve in your relationship to keep this conflict unresolved?

For those who seek resolution, this final phase can be a vulnerable and challenging time. It requires a willingness to share openly and honestly about what led to the conflict and what needs to be done differently in the future. This can be a stretch for many couples, but it's also an opportunity to strengthen the bond between you.

When you're able to find a mutually beneficial solution, you may feel a sense of relief and forward progress. The gift of hope that comes with resolution can bring a renewed sense of purpose to your relationship. By embracing the post-conflict phase as an opportunity for growth and learning, you can deepen your emotional connection and build a stronger, more resilient relationship.

WHAT CAN I DO IN THE RETURN TO STATUS QUO OR RESOLUTION PHASE?

This phase is the "fork in the road." You have two choices, and your decisions, over time, will shape the destiny of your marriage. If you don't want to work out the core of the problem and make it so both of you are content, you can keep on having the same debates but never quite get to a solution, go back to how things were before, and pretend everything is okay. While this might seem like a good idea in the short term, it's important to remember that continuing this way will mean these arguments start coming up more often.

OR

You can get radical and address what brought the two of you to this point and truly work to create a different outcome in the future. You can seek to understand your feelings and your spouse's feelings. You can choose to implement different strategies when it comes to how the two of you handle your feelings and conflict in your marriage. You can develop different reactions and take new action steps in order to change the cycle.

Getting to a true resolution takes a willingness to see things from your spouse's point of view. It's looking at what's best for your marriage and not just what's best for you. Resolution is a learned skill. It takes practice. It takes courage. You can choose to do conflict differently.

As you seek to build more conflict resolution in your marriage, use the framework of the 6 Pillars of Intimacy®. This framework was designed to help the two of you stay connected. When there are cracks in any of the pillars, you find yourself in conflict and feeling disconnected. By being able to identify what pillar has a crack in it, you are taking the first step toward finding the resolution. You are giving the problem an identity. Most people can't take action on the things they aren't aware of. But when you bring awareness to your marriage, you can take baby steps toward addressing one pillar of intimacy at a time in your marriage. You don't need big steps; a little goes a long way.

LOOKING AT YOUR CYCLES SIDE-BY-SIDE

Now it's time to look at each of your workbook pages side-by-side with your spouse. When I am coaching couples, I will lay these pages side-by-side to see the conflict cycle patterns that emerge. It's powerful to see how each spouse feels in each phase of the conflict cycle. When you see your cycle diagrammed on paper, you regain your power over the conflict. From there you can create strategies that will work. When the two of you individually take the time to complete the conflict cycle and internal conflict cycle, you bring awareness to your marriage. This allows you to identify the swirling emotions and look for opportunities to interrupt the cycle.

These amazing gaps from one stage to the next in the cycle represent your opportunities to interrupt and prioritize the marriage, the connection, and the intimacy. It may be a bit clunky the first time, but it doesn't take long before you are able to do this like a pro. If you slip and fall back in the cycle, take time later to diagram the conflict and see where things went wrong:

- Where did you diverge and move in different directions?
- What did you see and hear in your spouse that escalated the situation for you?
- What did you think and feel inside yourself that took the conflict to the next level?
- What can you do when you become aware of what *you* are processing at the start of a conflict? Or what *your spouse* is feeling?
- What can you do differently when you know what your conflict cycle is?
- Where can the two of you intentionally interrupt the cycle to get to a resolution faster?

CHAPTER 6

THE WHAT, WHEN, WHERE, AND WHY OF OUR CONFLICT CYCLE

Change is painful, but nothing is as painful as staying stuck somewhere you don't belong.

———

Mandy Hale

In the last chapter, you learned how to diagram a conflict cycle in your marriage. Understanding your cycles and where there are gaps that you can interrupt is important. It is also important to look at a few other key areas to help you break or interrupt the cycle faster. Tony and I still have conflict in our marriage, it's our awareness not only of the cycle but the factors in this chapter that help us resolve the conflict faster with less damage to our relationship.

WHAT HAVE BEEN OUR MOST EFFECTIVE STRATEGIES WHEN IT COMES TO HANDLING CONFLICT?

Just because you are reading a book on conflict doesn't mean you don't already have some things worked out. Maybe you've already figured out a strategy or several strategies that work when dealing with certain conflicts. If you have, you can apply these to new situations as they arise. If you haven't thought of these before, they can be great tools to add to your marriage toolbox. Some examples of strategies:

- "Big" or "heavy" conversations don't happen after 9 pm (or another set time) because you recognize you will likely be too tired for the conversation to be effective. Instead, the two of you schedule a time to talk about the challenges you are facing. This strategy works to find a time when you are both at your best for conversations instead of being fatigued or overwhelmed.
- You've learned to be specific about what the problem is so the two of you can get on the same team in finding solutions for the challenge instead of attacking one another. Doing this allows

the two of you to focus on the problem and not make the other person the problem.

- Before you go to your spouse with your feelings or emotions, you take time to reflect on what's going on with you so you can be proactive instead of reactive. This strategy empowers you to experience your emotions and develop the ability to discuss them.

- You've identified that having conversations about certain topics in certain rooms never seems to go well so you choose to have those conversations in a different location. By doing this, the two of you deal with challenges in environments that are more neutral and less emotionally charged.

- You recognize that after you share something with your spouse, it's helpful to give them time to process it before continuing the conversation. One of my coaching clients shares what they want to talk about and then they agree to wait 20-30 minutes before discussing it as a couple so they can process their feelings. This strategy demonstrates respect for your spouse and acknowledges that being reactive generally doesn't go well for most couples.

- The two of you have a "code" word. A code word is spoken to indicate a timeout, a break in the conversation, or the choice to interrupt the conflict cycle. This code word can be called by either spouse to identify that something is off. It's not an accusation that the other person is "misbehaving." Rather, it's a tool used to say, "When this pattern starts, we tend to behave in a way that isn't great for us. Let's pause and regroup before things get worse." The code word can be just about anything, but it helps if it's a neutral word or a word that is funny.

When you know something works in an area of conflict or pillar of intimacy, it's important to look at how it can work in another area of your marriage. Skills are skills—use the ones you have to break the conflict cycle in your marriage.

WHEN ARE WE MOST LIKELY TO EXPERIENCE CONFLICT?

Just as you have rhythms in your personal and professional life, there are rhythms in your marriage. By identifying the rhythms when you are most likely to experience conflict, you can take preventative measures to reduce the conflict in your marriage. Ask yourself:

- Does fatigue play a role in our conflict? Do we seem to always be fighting after a long day of work or raising the children? Do our schedules keep us from being awake and able to handle challenges?

  Solution: *Schedule time each week to talk about the challenges the two of you are facing, individually or as a couple. Knowing there is time to talk about what needs to be addressed can minimize the need for those late-night conversations that seem to go nowhere.*

- Is there a time of the day, week, or month that we are more likely to experience conflict? "Time of the month" has nothing to do with a woman's menstrual cycle, although for some couples these hormonal changes may lead to more conflict. In some marriages, the end of the month, when there's "more month than money" can be a source of conflict. For others, it may be when there are lots of days off with the kids or even after a weekend spent running errands or being with family.

Solution: *When you recognize that certain periods of the day, week, or month can be challenging for your relationship, don't wait until then to reach out to your spouse. Make sure both of you are aware of the changes in each other's lives and discuss them proactively. It's always better to plan ahead rather than deal with issues when they arise.*

- Are there day-to-day pressures that lend themselves to conflict? Do you find the busyness of your days or the obligations you have lead to more conflict? Are there activities you need to reduce so you have more bandwidth for your marriage?

Solution: *What can you say "no" to? Where can you reduce your commitments? If you have too many things on your plate, this can leave you feeling overwhelmed or stressed. Too much stress and overwhelm are a recipe for conflict. Work together as a team to come up with creative strategies to reduce the busyness of your days.*

- Are you more stressed around payday or does bill day heighten the tension? Finances play a huge role in creating conflict in a lot of marriages. If this is the case in yours, how can the two of you get on the same team to handle things differently?

Solution: *Create a money plan to help reduce the challenges around paydays or days when bills are due. Working together to reduce conflict around finances and be on the same page is a great way to reduce the overall conflict in your marriage.*

These are all times when your personal emotional state could be heightened or depleted, making you more susceptible to conflict. Being aware of these times allows you as an individual and as a couple, to be proactive, instead of reactive. You can take action to increase connection in a meaningful way in the 6 Pillars of Intimacy® to reduce tension and minimize conflict.

WHERE ARE WE MOST LIKELY TO EXPERIENCE CONFLICT AND HOW CAN WE CHANGE THAT LOCATION?

What is the place where conflicts are most likely to come up between you and your spouse? I touched on this when discussing successful strategies, but now let's go deeper.

From my work with couples, I have found that certain spots tend to be more conflict-prone than others. Why? Because you have patterns of having the same conversations in the same places and muscle memory takes over. In other words, you go on autopilot and move into a place where you are just responding instead of actively engaging with your spouse. In the kitchen or around the dining table, disagreements about parenting may arise. Finances can be a source of tension in the home office. Issues about Sexual Intimacy may happen in the bedroom. Quarrels about praying together or attending services might take place in the car on the way to church. Anywhere both of you are can become a battleground for disagreement.

Once you know these patterns, you can do something to modify your behavior and the environment. Changing location will alter how you naturally respond to each other's words and actions; by doing so, it breaks the loop of repeating similar conversations in the same spot. The room, people around, and even your tone of voice can all change when you change locations.

WHY DOES IT MATTER THAT YOU DEVELOP THE SKILLS TO BREAK YOUR CONFLICT CYCLE?

Stop for a minute and ask yourself these questions:

- Why does breaking our conflict cycle matter?
- Why do I/we want to change our patterns?

When you recognize that how the two of you do marriage and conflict, impacts those around you and the environment you live in, you can develop a deep motivation to change your actions. See, when you break the cycle of negative conflict patterns, it not only helps your marriage but also sets a good example for your children. They can develop healthy conflict resolution skills, which will help them in their own relationships and change this cycle for future generations.

Breaking the conflict cycle can make your marriage more fulfilling and happy. When you learn how to communicate effectively and resolve conflicts in a healthy way, you can strengthen your emotional connection with your partner and create a more loving and supportive relationship. And when your home is more peaceful, this will positively impact other areas of your life. You will feel more grounded emotionally and better able to handle challenges at work and in your community. It's a ripple effect—when your marriage is a place of peace and safety, other areas of your life become easier.

Write down your why! Keep it visible and handy so you can refer back to it when the two of you find yourselves in conflict. These "whys" are important. You aren't breaking the conflict cycle "just because" you are on a mission to do marriage differently.

TONY'S THOUGHTS

Why is it important that Alisa and I do conflict well? Why do we try to have big conversations before 9 pm? Why do we try to clear our calendars from time to time? The answer to all of these questions is our relationship is *that* important. When I married Alisa, I said I do to her as part of our vows. Those two words are the reason that we keep striving to do conflict better.

After more than two decades of marriage, I realize that wanting to have an extraordinary marriage doesn't "just happen," but rather it's the result of being intentional in every pillar of intimacy. This means I have to keep growing, even when it's hard. I have to learn what I am doing well in the relationship and where I need to improve. I don't ever want Alisa and me to fall into a place where we've just settled for good enough. If that means we have to have hard conversations, we have the hard conversations.

> It's given me the language to be able to tell Alisa how I see the problems without making her be the problem.

Building our marriage on the framework of the 6 Pillars of Intimacy®, allows us to be specific about the challenges we are facing so we can focus on the problem. It's given me the language to be able to tell Alisa how I see the problems without making her be the problem. You may find many of your fights center around the same set of issues. Next, we will look at how to solve some of the recurring or common conflicts in each of the 6 Pillars of Intimacy®.

CHAPTER 7

COMMON CONFLICT CHALLENGES IN THE 6 PILLARS OF INTIMACY®

All things are difficult before they are easy.

Thomas Fuller

Throughout this book, I have offered tactics and methods to assist you in recognizing your responses to conflicts, recognizing patterns detrimental to your marriage, and establishing new habits that could benefit how you manage conflicts in the future. Many of my coaching clients have told me that understanding the 6 Pillars of Intimacy® has helped them in resolving their negative conflict cycles and improving their connection. When you are able to understand these components of a good relationship, it opens up a discussion between the two of you on what is functioning well and what needs to be improved. This can serve as an excellent starting point when trying to address specific issues and come up with solutions.

As I share with you how to manage conflicts in each pillar, it's important to keep in mind the objective isn't to eliminate all conflict, *conflict is a part of marriage*, rather it's to learn how to go through conflict in a manner that will bring you closer together and promote intimacy.

Emotional Intimacy is your closeness and connection through your verbal and nonverbal communication. So, if you find the two of you are struggling with conflict like this:

- Conversations only about the kids/work/chores:
  - Set up times to talk about those particular topics AND other times to talk about topics that excite each of you, such as your dreams and passions.
  - Use tools like conversation starter cards, which you can find on Amazon, or our book, *Connect Like You Did When You First Met: 101 Proven Questions for Couples* at https://ConnectLikeYouDid.com, to change up the topics you talk about.

- Remember when you were first getting to know one another? Curiosity and wonder are important tools for both of you no matter how long you've been married.
- Not sharing feelings:
  - Use a tool like an emotion wheel to explore feelings words. This tool and many like it can be found by doing a Google search for "Emotion Wheel." Typically, in the center of the wheel are the six most common emotions and the second and third levels of the wheel enable you to go deeper into the emotions you or your spouse are feeling. By using the words on the wheel, you can gain clarity on what you or your spouse are feeling in a more tangible way.
  - Embrace the idea that change is possible. Just because you weren't raised "like that" doesn't mean you cannot develop the skill. Many clients over the years have shared "I'm not a talker," "I just don't communicate well," or "I never learned to talk about my feelings." Just because you didn't doesn't mean you can't. I've worked with folks in their 50s and 60s who have developed skills to communicate with their spouse. If they can do it, so can you.
  - Evaluate when and where the two of you discuss feelings, you might need to implement being in a different location or talking at a different time of day. Too often, certain rooms or certain times of day can cause one or both of you to retreat. Maybe it's too late at night or maybe you always talk about money

at the kitchen table… in either case, finding a better time of day or different location can break the patterns of behavior.

- Blow up or turn ice cold:
  - These are learned behaviors. Evaluate what causes you to default to these behaviors. Identify what you can do to create different reactions in yourself. Getting too hot for your spouse to handle or too cold for them to approach, can be changed. You know yourself better than anyone. What causes you to react that way and what can you do to release that energy before it harms you *and your spouse?*
  - When the internal alarm bells start ringing, what can you do differently? Your body is wired to notify you that there's been a change in the environment. When the alarms sound, how will you choose to implement the code word or ask for space so the conflict doesn't become detrimental to the marriage?

Physical Intimacy is your closeness and connection in non-sexual touch. When you find yourself in conflict over…

- Not giving enough touch:
  - Have the conversation about what touches are meaningful, then work to touch your spouse in a way that is meaningful *to them.* Just because that might not be the way you would want to be touched doesn't make it unimportant. It's always interesting to see when meaningful touches are given and received, the conflict around this diminishes.

- Understand that one spouse may need gentle reminders. Devise a strategy so this can be done without feeling like a nag—no one wants to be a nag or be nagged. What can the two of you agree on as a reminder? Is it like Tony who will simply say in the car, "I like it when you rest your hand on my leg?" Or will it be something like, "Let's make sure to kiss every time one of us leaves or comes home?"
- Develop a system to communicate about touch. Is this part of a weekly check-in? Is there a code word the two of you will use to indicate that touch is desired? Remember touch is important. Finding a way to meet the needs of both spouses is a gift to your marriage.
- Touch only ever leads to sex:
  - Have a conversation on the differences between Physical and Sexual Intimacy. Get clear, as a couple, on touches that are for Physical Intimacy and touches for Sexual Intimacy.
  - Evaluate why this is the case in your marriage. What circumstances have led to Physical Intimacy being associated with Sexual Intimacy? Determine what you can do to change this association. It may be necessary to state, "I'm touching you in this way with no expectation of Sexual Intimacy" in order to break the mental cycle of certain touches only being associated with Sexual Intimacy.
  - Make a plan to build Physical Intimacy in your marriage. Remember, for most couples the "get to know you" phase was often

marked with hugs, kisses, hand-holding, and other non-sexual activities. Those are *still* good for your relationship.

- One of you is able to be physically affectionate with the kids or friends but not with your spouse:
    - Make time to be husband and wife and touch as spouses or lovers. Yes, the roles of mom and dad are important. It is critical your children know they are loved and experience affection from you. However, research indicates that your attention and affection toward one another, as spouses, is just as important to the security, well-being, and development of your children. Your affection sets them up for success in their future.
    - Recognize that touch changes after children and that it's still important. Many mothers, especially those of young children, will lament that by the end of the day, they feel "all touched out." It's not unexpected given the physical needs of your children. This is where rediscovering meaningful touches can be so instrumental in reducing conflict and building connection.
    - Address other pillars of intimacy to reduce conflict about Physical Intimacy. Are the two of you spending time together (Recreational Intimacy)? What is the nature of your conversations (Emotional Intimacy)? Do you make time to pray together (Spiritual Intimacy)? As you build the other pillars of intimacy, you can create natural or spontaneous moments of Physical Intimacy.

Financial Intimacy is the connection built from discussing every financial aspect of your marriage. Do you fight over...

- Secret spending:
    - Why does one or both of you hide your spending? What are the emotions tied to those purchases? What did you learn about keeping purchasing hidden as you were growing up? The answers to these questions can often indicate why the conflict is happening and can be used to build connection in the marriage.
    - Work with a coach or mentor to understand why you or your spouse doesn't feel comfortable being transparent about spending. There are likely cracks in the Emotional Intimacy pillar that are leading to the secrets or not feeling safe to be transparent.
    - Establish regular money meetings in your marriage to evaluate what's going out and what's coming in. Consistency in these meetings and the review of your accounts brings a higher level of transparency to your marriage and builds the team aspect of your marriage thus reducing the conflict.
- Spending too much:
    - Who is spending the money and why? What have been the conversations around spending? It's important to get to a place of curiosity and understanding in order to create a strategy. Are there habits like gambling or a shopping addiction that need to be professionally addressed? If so, get the professional help you need to reduce this conflict in your marriage.

- Establish spending thresholds. Many of the couples I work with who are experiencing conflicts in Financial Intimacy will implement a spending threshold, an amount that if a purchase exceeds it, the two of them will have a conversation before purchasing. This brings the two of you together to discuss finances around larger purchases in order to reduce friction when one person spends too much.
- Create separate accounts for household budgetary needs and "fun" money. This strategy pays for the household needs first and then puts an agreed-upon amount into a separate account for each of you. That money can be spent as you wish.

- One spouse NOT being involved in family finances:
  - What are the expectations each of you has when it comes to participating in the family finances? What did you see growing up and how is this mirrored in your marriage? Just because your parents did it one way doesn't mean that is the right way for your relationship.
  - What skills or knowledge do you need to be able to participate? If you don't feel competent discussing finances, what knowledge do you need? It's OK to say, "I don't understand that," or "I don't know what that means." But that's not an excuse to stay uninvolved in your finances. In this day of Google and YouTube, you can get the answers to just about anything financially related.

- What would it look like for both of you to be involved in the finances? Dream for a minute about a conversation in which you both participated and felt good about the interaction. What did you do? What did you say? Start there to build the skills you need to reduce conflict in this area.

Spiritual Intimacy is the way you are close and connected through your religious beliefs and observed religious practices. Are you fighting over…

- Not praying together:
  - What are the expectations around a couple praying together? What would build one's confidence in being able to do this? Most people have never been taught how to pray together and it can feel awkward to start this new activity. It can also feel very vulnerable. You don't have to be perfect. You don't have to know all the right words. You simply have to try.
  - When does it make sense for the two of you to pray together? Some couples try to do it first thing in the morning or as the last thing before bed. If you are like me and Tony, neither of those times of day work for us. It's OK to find another time. Some of my clients pray in the car when it's just the two of them and others pray when they feel conflict starting. You can make the rules for your marriage.
  - Who can you learn from about praying together as a couple? You don't have to figure it out on your own. If you didn't grow up seeing couples pray you may not even know

what this could look like in your marriage, you just have a sense that you *should* do it. Ask other couples what it looks like for them. You can learn so much from those conversations on how you can do this together.

- Not attending services together:
  - Why don't you attend services together? Is it scheduling? Is it a difference of beliefs? Is it difficult to take the kids? Is it the church? There can be a lot of reasons why a couple doesn't attend services together and getting to the root can help you look for those win-win solutions to make it happen.
  - What are the expectations each of you has and how can you build a plan that honors each of your expectations? Some spouses never went to church as a kid or never saw their parents go to church. Some families only went to services on holidays, while others went every weekend or whenever the church was open. Learning to discuss your expectations and working to find a solution that honors both of you, can take some work but it can also reduce conflict in this area. Remember, while faith is an individual journey, Spiritual Intimacy is a way to be connected to your spouse in this area.
- Not willing to do a devotional:
  - What has kept the two of you from doing this together? Time of day? Type of devotional? Frequency? Talk about it. In the early years of our marriage, Tony and I tried to get up early and do a devotional every morning. More often than not, we hit snooze instead

of getting up. We eventually realized it was better for us to do it at the end of the day. What works for the two of you? You get to make the rules.

- How could this benefit your marriage? Sometimes conflict can arise when you don't have an understanding of how something will benefit the two of you, you only hear the request to do it. Have a discussion about the possible benefits. Keep trying until you find a rhythm that works for your marriage.

Recreational Intimacy is how you grow your closeness and connection by spending time together and making memories. Is the conflict around...

- Never going on dates:
  - What are the barriers to going on dates and what can you do to minimize those barriers? Is it child care? Not knowing what to do? Not having a lot of money or time? All of those can be worked through when the two of you sit down and make a plan. One of the easiest ways to do this is to create a list of ideas, based on your current circumstances, that could be considered dates. Once you have the list, you can start making your dates happen.
  - How do you define a "date?" Can you have a date at home or do you have to go out? Is it a date if you do something during the day or is it only a date if you go out at night? Do you consider it a date if you take the kids with you? The answers to these questions and the actions you take based on those answers can help to reduce conflict in this intimacy.

- Only one of you plans the dates:
  - Does the person who is **not** planning the dates feel confident or capable? What would make both of you feel confident in planning dates? Would it be helpful to have a list of date ideas? The babysitter's phone number? Best days of the week for dates? When you are both equipped with ideas for dates, childcare help (if needed), and the ability to schedule things on your calendar, you'll find that you can minimize conflict.
  - Have you often said the dates your spouse plans are not good or you don't want to go on "that type of date?" Most spouses will do more of what they are praised for and less of what they are criticized for. This is especially true when it comes to planning dates. How can you change your words to create a space where this is not a source of conflict but rather an opportunity to grow in your marriage?
- Dates are always the same thing:
  - What does it look like for the two of you to create an idea list so you aren't doing the same thing? Nowhere is it written that every date has to be dinner and a movie. Doing something different brings anticipation and excitement to dates. Create a list of dates you've never done. Make a commitment to try a new place or activity for at least every other date—this way you can still do some of your old favorites and try new things.
  - What can you do to bring variety into the time of day or location of your dates? As the seasons in your life change, you may find

what you've been doing doesn't work in the current season. Changing things up based on work schedules or kids' schedules can help the two of you break out of the routine. It's OK to go out for breakfast instead of dinner or go out during the day instead of at night. When you introduce variety, you minimize the conflict.

Sexual Intimacy is everything about your sexual connection with your spouse. Do you fight over...

- One of you always initiating:
  - Does the person who **doesn't** initiate feel comfortable or confident in doing so? What would help him/her develop confidence in initiating? There can be a lot of beliefs about who should initiate or what initiating looks like. It's important to know everyone has a deep need to feel desired and initiating is one way to express to your spouse that you see and desire them. If you don't know how to initiate or feel confident in doing so, recognize that you can learn. There are many resources out there with great ideas. You'll need to practice though. It might not go smoothly the first time around. Keep trying as this can eliminate the conflict around this frustration.
  - Do you know how your spouse initiates? This is a real conversation to have. For years, Tony didn't know how I initiated and when I did, he didn't get the hint and I felt rejected.

> Confusion often creates conflict but clarity brings connection.

It was a serious cycle of conflict. Having this type of conversation makes it so much easier to reduce the conflict and enjoy Sexual Intimacy. Tell your spouse the specific actions you'll take to initiate. Confusion often creates conflict but clarity brings connection.

- What does it look like for both of you to initiate in your marriage? When one of you doesn't initiate, Sexual Intimacy can feel very one-sided and the spouse who does initiate may begin to question if they are desired. This questioning can create conflict in the marriage. With the frequency of your love-making, will you take turns initiating? Will it be some other system? You get to decide!

- Sex is always the same thing:
  - What are the mindsets around Sexual Intimacy and variety when it comes to sex? The messages you received about sex: how it's done, what the purpose is, who sex is for—all of these play into what happens in your bedroom. What did you learn growing up and how is that impacting how you show up now? One of the things I've realized as a coach is identifying these mindsets is the first step to reducing conflict in this area.

  > If your life is so busy that your spouse doesn't show up on your calendar, you are going to have conflict in your Sexual Intimacy.

  - What is the resistance to trying something

new? Variety brings excitement and anticipation to your Recreational Intimacy. It does
the same in your Sexual Intimacy. It's important to explore the areas of resistance in order to create a plan to reduce conflict.

- Have the discussion about trying new things
  away from the bedroom and especially not
  right before the two of you might be about to
  have sex. The timing and location, as I have
  discussed earlier in the book, can actually
  create more conflict.

- Differences in desire:
  - Is there a medical reason for this? Get your
    hormones checked. You have no idea how
    many coaching sessions have been about
    conflict arising from differences in desire.
    Find yourself a doctor/clinic that specializes
    in hormones, not just running bloodwork.
    Your hormones run everything and if they
    aren't functioning at optimal levels *for you,*
    the low desire or high desire definitely cre-
    ates cycles of conflict.
  - When was the last time you truly romanced
    one another? Do you even know how to ro-
    mance your spouse? Everyone I work with
    wants to be seen, valued, and cherished by
    their spouse. However, laziness and busyness
    often get in the way. Ask your spouse, "How
    do you like to be romanced?" Don't assume
    you know. When you get an answer, begin to
    implement that action. Feeling romanced is a
    great way to build desire.
  - Implement a tool like the Intimacy Lifestyle
    to "take the guesswork out of knowing when

you are going to get some." Back to those busy schedules. The Intimacy Lifestyle is a tool Tony and I devised to help ourselves, and other couples, determine both frequency and shared initiation of Sexual Intimacy—two of the biggest sources of conflict in this area. By discussing and implementing a plan for the two of you, you can greatly reduce the conflict in this area. If your life is so busy that your spouse doesn't show up on your calendar, you are going to have conflict in your Sexual Intimacy. Put your marriage, and especially your sex life, on the calendar.

What you've just read has been a sampling of the many conflicts I've witnessed over the years in coaching sessions. They are by no means exhaustive. Rather, I've shared them with you to demonstrate that there are ways to approach the challenging areas. Ask yourself and your spouse questions and then come up with a plan or a strategy to create change.

Set yourself up for success. Don't try to do a complete overhaul and expect it to be perfect. Trying to do too much at once and expecting perfection is only going to frustrate you, *and likely lead to more conflict.* Instead, focus on baby steps: Little actions you can do consistently over time to effect big changes. There are lots of options when it comes to your baby steps. Some you can start with:

- Pick one step in the conflict cycle and change your action or reaction.
- Choose one pillar of intimacy and focus on those conflicts or challenges instead of trying to address all of the conflict in your marriage at the same time.

- Be mindful of the words you speak and your tone of voice.
- Stay aware of your patterns. Awareness is a preemptive behavior. When you stay focused on what's caused problems in the past, you can choose different actions in the future.

Change in conflict is possible—if you are willing to change your actions and reactions. It is a choice. And it's one you have to make as you think through your next steps.

CHAPTER 8

WHAT'S YOUR NEXT STEP?

When a marriage works, nothing on earth can take its place.

———

Helen Gahagan

Here you are at the end of the book. You have re-flected on what your conflict cycle looks like, what you often fight about, and even what you experience internally when the two of you are in conflict. You've looked at each of the 6 Pillars of Intimacy® and thought about which of these are often the source of conflict in your marriage. You've started thinking about the strategies you could deploy to break the conflict cycle and move toward more conflict resolution.

As a marriage coach, my job is to ask you, what's your next step? No coach wants to see a person stay in the exact same spot they started in. And, to be truthful, I didn't write this book for you to do nothing.

So, what is next for you and the way you do conflict in your marriage?

OPTION 1: I READ THE BOOK, I'M GOOD

For those of you who choose this option, in just a couple of pages, you'll finish the book and think to yourself, "I'm good, I know what I need to know so I don't need to do anything else." If that's you, know I am cheering you on and praying for the shifts in your conflict resolution. Here's something you should know and something I tell my coaching clients regularly, "Nothing changes in a marriage until the actions change."

Having knowledge alone is not enough; you must take action based on that knowledge. As of the writing of this book, a Google search for the term "conflict resolution" yielded 389,000,000 results. That's a lot of information and yet conflict is still an issue for countless couples. If you only read this book and choose to do the "same old, same old" in your marriage, you will get the same results you've already gotten. In other words, not much will change.

OPTION 2: WE'RE WRITING A NEW CHAPTER IN OUR MARRIAGE

Some of you see the end of this book as the beginning of a new chapter in your marriage, a chapter where you don't do the same old dance I described in Chapter 1. For those of you starting a new chapter and taking new actions in conflict resolution... I can't wait to see the beautiful new dance the two of you do! As you go forward:

- Evaluate your conflict cycles whenever you feel stuck. Print out a fresh copy of the workbook when the two of you find yourselves in negative conflict patterns and work to look for interruptions. Remember that you get to choose a new response in every conflict and in every phase of the conflict cycle. Always be thinking, "What can I do differently here?"
- Use the 6 Pillars of Intimacy® as a framework to address the conflicts in your marriage. By identifying the specific pillar and actions that cause conflict, you and your spouse can create a plan to overcome these issues and build unity.

OPTION 3: WE NEED HELP

Some of you may be looking at what you learned in this book and the dance you do and are thinking, "I don't know how we are going to change our dance. I understand what needs to change, but it feels like what we do is too ingrained. We don't know how to break the cycles on our own." If this is you, it's time to get a marriage instructor or coach.

Extraordinary dancers have an instructor, a coach who helps them learn; someone who holds them accountable to the excellence they want to achieve. What's true in dance is also true in marriage. Extraordinary results do not happen by chance; they are the result of intentional action and accountability. A marriage coach helps the two of you perfect your most extraordinary marriage dance—without stepping on each other's toes.

As a coach, I help couples break their ineffective cycles. When a couple invites me into their marriage, I have the ability to take the 30,000-foot view and help couples identify what they are doing and guide them as they make the changes necessary to create new, healthy patterns.

It can be extremely hard when you are in the midst of the conflict to see what other options exist. The two of you can be so entrenched in your patterns you literally can't see what else you could do. There is no shame in saying you need help to change or that you can't do it by yourself. In fact, I'm often overwhelmed by the courage coaching clients demonstrate when it comes to taking action and making changes in their marriages.

You can break the conflict cycles in your relationship and build the extraordinary marriage you desire. Choosing to learn how to have a successful marriage and resolve conflict is a decision. So, as you finish this book, what's your next step? Is it time for the two of you to choose to do conflict well and learn how to create an extraordinary marriage? I believe the answer is YES! I can't wait to see what the two of you accomplish as you break the conflict cycles in your marriage. Grant yourselves permission to learn these concepts, develop new skills, and resolve conflict effectively.

You can do this!

Love you guys.

ACKNOWLEDGEMENTS

Every book I write is a testament to the gifts that God has given me. I'm grateful for the burden He has placed on my heart to impact one marriage. Both Tony and I get up every day with that mission.

Thank you to my friends who kept asking when the book was going to get done. You kept me accountable when I didn't think I wanted to finish it, when I wondered if it would make a difference.

I am beyond thankful for my Friday morning Bible study group. Your prayers and revelations have given me so much strength and hope. Your reminders about the impact this book would have on couples around the world pushed me through daunting moments when I was stuck.

To the Balboa Season 11 Pathfinders apprentices, your enthusiasm was incredibly validating when I shared these concepts with you, pushing me to include insights from our time together.

To all my coaching clients—thank you for allowing me to witness the transformations in your marriages. It takes a lot of courage to ask for help and be open to receiving it. The insights gained in our sessions have had an immense influence on this book. Your vulnerability will make a difference in the lives of so many other marriages.

And lastly, I would like to thank the one person who has been with me since 1994—Tony. You had to push me harder than ever to finish this book, and I know I didn't make it easy. Thank you for having the hard conversations with me, and always pushing forward in a loving way whenever I needed that extra nudge. And also, thank you for all the hard work it takes to turn every idea into a printed page. I couldn't do any of this without you—and I wouldn't want to.

DO YOU NEED PERSONAL HELP TO IMPROVE YOUR MARRIAGE?

It starts with YOU. Not your spouse. I've had several incredible coaching calls with spouses who realized this.

The changes beginning to occur in this marriage, because one person decided to make a change, are amazing.

If you want things to change, change first; work on what you CAN do.

See if marriage coaching is right for you. Click the link below to Apply for Marriage Coaching today!

oneextraordinarymarriage.com/coaching

ABOUT THE AUTHORS

Tony and Alisa DiLorenzo are sought-after speakers, podcast hosts, and coaches on the topics of sex, love, and marriage. They share the hardships and triumphs they have had in their marriage through their site at ONE Extraordinary Marriage. Through their stories, energy, and passion, they inspire every couple to live an extraordinary marriage.

Having dealt with the issues of pornography, financial crisis, and child loss, they understand the issues that impact relationships and trust. They work with couples around the world, equipping them with the tools and strategies they need to rebuild broken trust.

Tony and Alisa have been featured on FOX News, The Chalene Show, Ask Dr. Drew, The Guardian, ESPN Radio, Lifestyle Magazine, Good Housekeeping, and MSN Living. They are the authors of several best-selling books, including The 6 Pillars of Intimacy: The Secret to an Extraordinary Marriage. Their podcast, ONE Extraordinary Marriage Show, is consistently the top marriage podcast on Apple Podcasts, with an audience around the world.

LEAVE A REVIEW

Love this book? Don't forget to let others know.

Every review matters, and it matters a lot!

Head over to your favorite online bookstore or wherever you purchased The 6 Pillars of Intimacy Conflict Resolution: The Secret to Breaking the Conflict Cycle in Your Marriage to leave an honest review for us.

We're truly honored and blessed to have you as part of the ONE Family.

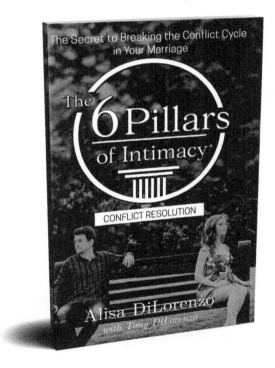

NOTES

If You Think It's Abuse
1. Power and Control. The Hotline. (2021, November 29). Retrieved January 27, 2023, from https://www.thehotline.org/identify-abuse/power-and-control/

Introduction
1. Scott, S. B., Rhoades, G. K., Stanley, S. M., Allen, E. S., & Markman, H. J. (2013, June). Reasons for Divorce and Recollections of Premarital Intervention: Implications for Improving Relationship Education. Couple & family psychology. Retrieved January 27, 2023, from https://www.ncbi.nlm.nih.gov/pmc/articles/PMC4012696/

Chapter 1: The Dance You Do
1. Merriam-Webster. (n.d.). *Conflict Definition & Meaning*. Merriam-Webster. Retrieved January 27, 2023, from https://www.merriam-webster.com/dictionary/conflict
2. *Marriage and Couples - Research*. The Gottman Institute. (2019, August 26). Retrieved February 8, 2023, from https://www.gottman.com/about/research/couples/
3. Askari, M., Noah, S., Hassan, S., & Baba, M. (2012, March 1). *Comparison the Effects of Communication and Conflict Resolution Skills Training on Marital Satisfaction*. International Journal of Psychological Studies. Retrieved February 2, 2023, from https://www.ccsenet.org/journal/index.php/ijps/article/view/6397

4. Wagner, A., Mossman, C. P., Scheeren, P., & Levandowski, D. C. (2019). *Conflict, Conflict Resolution and Marital Quality.* American Psychological Association. Retrieved January 6, 2023, from https://psycnet.apa.org/record/2019-58907-001

5. Staff. (2022). *Causes of Divorce: 13 of the Most Common Reasons.* Divorce.com. Retrieved January 6, 2023, from https://divorce.com/blog/causes-of-divorce/

6. DiLorenzo, A. (2021). Chapter 1: Challenge #1. In *The 6 Pillars of Intimacy*®: *The Secret to an Extraordinary Marriage* (p. 23). ONE Extraordinary Marriage.

Chapter 2: Know Thyself First

1. Rodgers, R., Andrews, J., Plummer, C., Hammerstein, O., Kostal, I., Haydn, R., Wood, P., Parker, E., Lehman, E., Lindsay, H., & Crouse, R. (1965). Do-Re-Mi. On *Rodgers and Hammerstein's The Sound of Music.* RCA Victor.

2. Acha, K. (2019, December 22). *Fight, Flight, Freeze Response to Stress & Conflict Resolution: Dr. Kenneth Acha.* Dr. Kenneth Acha | Habits for Life. Retrieved March 17, 2023, from https://www.kennethmd.com/fight-flight-freeze-response-to-stress-conflict-resolution/

3. Taylor, M. (2022, April 28). *Acute Stress Response: Fight, Flight, Freeze, and Fawn.* WebMD. Retrieved March 18, 2023, from https://www.webmd.com/mental-health/what-does-fight-flight-freeze-fawn-mean

4. *How to Overcome the Freeze Response.* NICABM. (2022, April 1). Retrieved March 18, 2023, from https://www.nicabm.com/topic/freeze/

Made in the USA
Las Vegas, NV
23 May 2023

72474164R00090